Selected Articles on Growing Pear Trees

by

Various

British Library Cataloguing-in-Publication Data
A catalogue record for this book is available from the
British Library

Fruit Growing

In botany, a fruit is a part of a flowering plant that derives from specific tissues of the flower, one or more ovaries, and in some cases accessory tissues. In common language use though, 'fruit' normally means the fleshy seed-associated structures of a plant that are sweet or sour, and edible in the raw state, such as apples, oranges, grapes, strawberries, bananas, and lemons. Many fruit bearing plants have grown alongside the movements of humans and animals in a symbiotic relationship, as a means for seed dispersal and nutrition respectively. In fact, humans and many animals have become dependent on fruits as a source of food. Fruits account for a substantial fraction of the world's agricultural output, and some (such as the apple and the pomegranate) have acquired extensive cultural and symbolic meanings. Today, most fruit is produced using traditional farming practices, in large orchards or plantations, utilising pesticides and often the employment of hundreds of workers. However, the yield of fruit from organic farming is growing – and, importantly, many individuals are starting to grow their own fruits and vegetables. This historic and incredibly important foodstuff is gradually making a come-back into the individual garden.

The scientific study and cultivation of fruits is called 'pomology', and this branch of methodology divides fruits into groups based on plant morphology and anatomy. Some of these useful subdivisions broadly incorporate 'Pome Fruits', including apples and pears, and 'Stone Fruits' so called because of their characteristic middle, including peaches, almonds, apricots, plums and cherries. Many hundreds of fruits, including fleshy fruits like apple, peach, pear, kiwifruit, watermelon and mango are commercially valuable as human food, eaten both fresh and as jams, marmalade and other preserves, as well as in other recipes. Because fruits have been such a major part of the human diet, different cultures have developed many varying uses for fruits, which often do not revolve around eating. Many dry fruits are used as decorations or in dried flower arrangements, such as lotus, wheat, annual honesty and milkweed, whilst ornamental trees and shrubs are often cultivated for their colourful fruits (including holly, pyracantha, viburnum, skimmia, beautyberry and cotoneaster).

These widespread uses, practical as well as edible, make fruits a perfect thing to grow at home; and dependent on location and climate – they can be very low-maintenance crops. One of the most common fruits found in the British countryside (and towns for that matter) is the blackberry bush, which thrives in most soils – apart from those which are poorly drained or mostly made of dry or sandy soil. Apple trees are, of course, are another classic and whilst they may take several years to grow into a well-established tree, they will grow nicely in most sunny and well composted areas. Growing one's own fresh, juicy tomatoes is one of the great pleasures of summer gardening, and even if the gardener doesn't have room for rows of plants, pots or hanging baskets are a fantastic solution. The types, methods and approaches to growing fruit are myriad, and far too numerous to be discussed in any detail here, but there are always easy ways to get started for the complete novice. We hope that the reader is inspired by this book on fruit and fruit growing – and is encouraged to start, or continue their own cultivations. Good Luck!

Contents

THE PEAR

NOT many of my readers will be inclined to quarrel with the assertion that the pear is the most delicious of our hardy tall fruits. There cannot be in life many more enjoyable experiences than that of consuming a well-ripened, well-grown Doyenne du Comice or Marie. Louise pear. It is not surprising, therefore, that interest in this fruit is keen and widespread: Most people wish to grow good pears.

THE CULTURAL PROGRAMME

The cultural programme is, in its main principles, so much like that of the apple that I need not do more than indicate the differences. That is why I have separated the two fruits. Types of tree, methods of planting, pruning and feeding are precisely the same. Seeing that the pear is the tenderer of the two, it is advisable, where there is a choice of site, to accord the favourable position to the pear. The trees blossom very early, so early, in fact, that sharp frost may normally occur at flowering time. For that reason an east aspect

1

A WELL-FLOWERED CORDON PEAR TREE
(INSET) THE PEAR SLUGWORM (A SERIOUS PEAR PEST)

should be avoided. South and south-west are the best. And where practicable, means should always be at hand for protecting blossoming trees. If frost threatens, cover them with a net or some light fabric such as tiffany. This can easily be done when the trees grow alongside a wall, while it is possible with bush trees of normal size in the open. The very tall specimens must, of course, be allowed to take their chance.

STOCKS
Every pear grower should buy his trees from a good nurseryman, thus making sure that they are on the right stocks. In normal times many pear trees are imported from the Continent. These are usually budded or grafted on to the De Fontenay stock, which under British conditions roots very weakly. Trees on this type are nearly always unsatisfactory.

The best type for bush and cordon trees is the Angers Quince, sometimes known as Malling Type A. It induces fairly vigorous rooting and a fruitful tree. There are one or two exceptions, including Marie Louise, Josephine de Malines and Souvenir du Congres. These varieties do not unite readily directly with a Quince stock, yet they give splendid returns on the Quince roots. To get over the difficulty of the imperfect union, the varieties mentioned are double budded or grafted, which means that a variety that takes perfectly to Quince, such as Pitmaston Duchess, is first worked on to it. When the union is complete, that variety is cut back to within a few inches of the Quince stock, and Marie Louise, Josephine de Malines and Souvenir du Congres are worked into it. These are points that should be carefully noted by the pear tree buyer.

Standard, half-standard and espalier trees are budded or grafted on to what are called free growing stocks. These are obtained from the seeds derived from Perry pummace. Of course, the seedlings are carefully selected, hence the reason why stock bought from an expert possesses such a clear advantage over others.

4

VARIETIES

Pears are not as sharply divided into culinary and dessert varieties as are apples. Most sorts are used for both purposes, though there are three kinds that are recognized as stewing pears only. These are Catillac, Vicar of Winkfield and Santa Claus. All can be used as soon as they are taken from the tree, and they will keep until the end of January. The following provide an excellent succession of first-class dessert pears which can, if desired, be used for stewing also. I give the season of use in parentheses after the name of the variety: Jargonelle (August), Williams' Bon Chretien (September), Beurré Diel (October and November), Conference (October and November), Louise Bonne of Jersey (October and November), Pitmaston Duchess (November and December), Beurré d'Anjou (November and December), Charles Ernest (December and January), Winter Nelis (December to March), Beurré Easter (January to March), and Josephine de Malines (January to April).

PEAR MATES

Some varieties of pear, like some varieties of apple, are self-sterile. It is advisable to note this point when planting. Amongst those given Conference and Jargonelle are self-fertile. The other varieties can be mated as follows : Williams' Bon Chretien with Louise Bonne of Jersey, Beurré Diel with Doyenne du Comice, Pitmaston Duchess with Catillac, Beurré d'Anjou with Beurré Easter, Charles Ernest with Vicar of Winkfield, Santa Claus with Josephine de Malines, and Winter Nelis with Pitmaston Duchess.

Pears should be gathered and stored in the manner advised for apples. The very greatest care should be taken in handling them, for they are easily bruised, and in a few hours a bruise becomes quite an extensive decay lesion. Though there is a certain amount of elasticity in the keeping season of apples, there is practically none in that of pears. When a fruit is ripe it must be eaten, and eaten quickly, or it will go wrong. Some of the

5

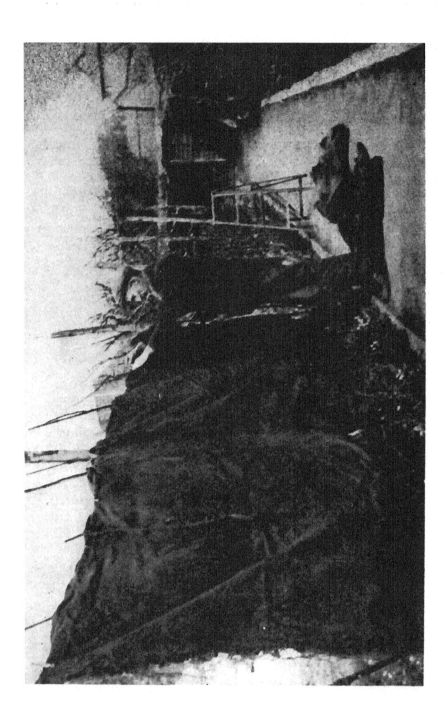

THE DELICIOUS DESSERT PEAR (MARIE LOUISE)

A CHOICE DESSERT PEAR (WILLIAMS' BON CHRETIEN)

A TEMPTING PICTURE. THE DESSERT PEAR (CONFERENCE)

WELL FRUITED YOUNG BUSH PEAR TREES

earlier varieties, such as Jargonelle, are ripe and mellow when taken from the tree. They should be consumed forthwith.

THE PEAR (continued)

PESTS AND DISEASES

THE pear is attacked by Aphides, Red Spider, Thrips, Winter Moth Caterpillars, and occasionally by American Blight and the larvæ of the Codlin Moth. In each case the preventive or remedial measures advised for the apple should be taken. In addition, this fruit is susceptible to attack by the special pests to be mentioned herewith.

THE PEAR MIDGE

A small two-winged fly appearing in April and May, and depositing her eggs in the blossoms. In a few days the eggs hatch into small, yellowish-white larvæ, which feed on the embryo fruits and spoil them. The larvæ pupate in the soil beneath the trees in June. If at this time naphthalene is raked in as far as the branches stretch, a good many of the larvæ will be destroyed. Infested fruits should be picked off and burned.

Where an attack has once occurred, it is not unreasonable to suppose that there will be a repetition. Some of the pupæ are sure to escape the soil fumigant. It then becomes necessary to spray with arsenate of lead just before the flower buds burst. This preparation is made by dissolving half a pound of arsenate of lead paste (containing 20 per cent of arsenic oxide) in ten gallons of water. The preparation is poisonous, therefore care should be taken not to allow it to drift on to vegetables.

LEAF BLISTER MITE

Sometimes the leaves on pear trees are disfigured by green, red or reddish-brown blisters. If one of these blisters is opened, and a magnifying glass is used, a number of tiny mites called Pear Leaf Blister Mites will be revealed. They are the cause of the eruptions, and the irritation may have a serious effect on the fertility of the tree. Occasionally the mites attack the fruits and cause them to shrivel up. They Winter in the bud scales, emerging in Spring to lay their eggs. This enemy can be destroyed by spraying with lime sulphur solution (one part in thirty parts of water) in December and, of course, the fallen leaves should be raked up and burned.

SOCIAL PEAR SAW-FLY

In several parts of the country the Social Pear Saw-fly is a pest to be reckoned with. This small fly lays her eggs in groups on the leaves, usually in early June. When the larvæ hatch, they don't separate, as most larvæ do, but remain in a colony, spinning a web for their own protection and feeding on the foliage. Owing to the presence of this web, it is quite impossible to do any good by spraying. The only practicable remedy is to detach the web and crush the caterpillars, or drop them into a pail of water.

PEAR DISEASES

Pears are susceptible to attack by Scab Disease, Canker. Brown Rot, and very occasionally Blossom Wilt Disease, Combat these enemies in the manner suggested for the apple. The only special disease that calls for mention is called Leaf Cluster Cups, which causes rugged swellings to appear on the upper surface of the leaves. On the under surface of the leaves there are flask-shaped bodies containing spores. Where this disease attacks the greater part of the foliage, as it often does, the tree is gravely weakened, and it usually becomes sterile. To obtain control, the tree should be sprayed with Bordeaux Mixture when the leaves have attained full size in Spring.

FRUIT GROWING

THE PEAR (*Pyrus communis*)

ORIGIN AND HISTORY

The pear, which is a member of the same genus as the apple, is a native of Britain. It is also indigenous to Europe and the more temperate parts of Asia. Under cultivation it yields one of our most delicious fruits, but its cultivation calls for careful study and attention if good results are to be obtained, as prevailing climate and conditions have a remarkable effect upon the fruit produced.

SOIL AND SITUATION

The best soil for all varieties of pear is a deep, well-drained medium loam of a " brick earth " type such as is found in the famous cherry districts of North Kent in the neighbourhood of Rainham, Sittingbourne and Faversham. The least suitable are shallow, light soils over chalk or gravel, and cold, badly-drained clays. Most varieties of pear tree can be grown in any good garden soil, but many of the best quality dessert pears, especially later-ripening varieties, can give satisfactory results only when grown in the milder districts of the south and west of England. These varieties are often shy croppers, do not mature properly on the tree, and for this reason are difficult to store. Hence they are seldom found in commercial plantations.

To produce some of these best quality late-keeping pears such as *Joséphine de Malines, Amiral Gervais*, or *Winter Nelis* on the table at their right season, and in perfect condition, is one of the most severe tests of skill in hardy fruit-growing in this country. For such varieties perfect shelter, a sunny position and a warm, dry ripening season are just as important as ideal soil. Unless *all* these conditions are obtainable, it is wise to avoid planting any but the more hardy varieties of mid-season pears. Fortunately, there are many of these which are less particular in their requirements, and which yet deserve to be described as high quality pears. *Laxton's Superb, Williams Bon Chrétien, Dr. Jules Guyot, Souvenir de Congrès, Beurré Hardy, Conference, Doyenné du Comice* and *Emile d'Heyst* are all grown to a certain extent in this country in commercial plantations where natural conditions are favourable. They should, therefore, be reasonably safe to recommend for any good garden conditions even in the colder districts of the north. At the bottom end of the scale are the very hardy varieties such as *Hessle, Chalk, Reine des Poires*, and *Fertility*, which can be grown under a fairly wide range of conditions, and in certain seasons will be found quite profitable at market, in spite of their poor flavour.

THE PEAR

It is useless to plant dessert pears in a north aspect, even against a wall, since abundance of sunshine and warmth is essential. One or two stewing varieties such as *Catillac* might succeed on a north wall. Shelter is, of course, required on the east and north. In the case of trees grown against walls, protection from frost may easily be afforded by hanging netting about 9 inches from the face of the wall as in the case of peaches and nectarines (see page 105).

FORMS OF TREES

Pears are naturally more slow to come into bearing than apples and require full exposure to the sun if their flavour is to be of the best. Hence they favour the more artificial forms of tree. In France, the land of pear-growing, the pyramid, the espalier, the fuseau, various forms of cordon, the single and double U, and many forms of candelabra and of palmette Verrier or " grid-irons," are all extensively used for the pear, the open bush or vase being one of the few forms which is seldom used. In this country the bush, cordon, espalier and grid-iron forms are the most popular. For garden trees of small and medium size, the single oblique cordon form is the cheapest to produce, and one of the most convenient to handle, but where space allows, the three- or four-tiered espalier is to be recommended. The standard and half-standard forms cannot be recommended for any but the most vigorous varieties such as *Pitmaston Duchess* or *Catillac*.

PROPAGATION

The pear is usually propagated by means of budding in the open in July and August, and by grafting in March and April, on pear or quince stocks. New varieties may be raised by means of seed, as described in Chapter IV, page 37.

ROOTSTOCKS FOR PEARS

Where space is limited and small trees of any form are required, a quince stock of unknown origin, sent to East Malling Research Station many years ago, and indexed there as *Quince C*, is to be recommended. Maiden trees on this stock are often inclined to be weak, but if planted in good soil and well-cared for, they will make sturdy, healthy little trees which come into cropping one, two, or even three years earlier than on any other known rootstock. For the next size of tree, as bush, pyramid, fuseau, espalier or grid-iron, or for cordons on poor soil, *Quince A*, known in this country as *Angers Quince*, and *Quince B*, or *Common Quince*, appear to be equally suitable rootstocks.

In the case of very weak-growing varieties such as *Olivier de Serres* to be trained as espaliers, for any form requiring strong extension growth, and for all varieties on *chalky* soils, the quince stocks cannot be recommended. In such cases a selected seedling pear stock should be used.

Incompatibility between Quince Stock and Pear Scion.—It has been found by experiment that when certain varieties of quince are used as rootstocks, most varieties of pear, when grafted or budded on them, fail to make good trees. There appears to be some form of incompatibility between the stock and scion as there is when apples are grafted on pears or vice versa.

In some cases the trees remain small and stunted, in others growth is normal for a few years and then suddenly in a gale the whole tree breaks off at the graft union. This phenomenon also occurs with plums on certain stocks. The best safeguard is to ensure that trees to be planted have been worked on one of the more compatible quince stocks such as A, B, or C. There are, however, some varieties of pear, such as *Dr. Jules Guyot* and *Williams Bon Chrétien*, which often show a certain degree of incompatibility when grafted or budded direct on'to any quince stocks. For such varieties the method known as "double-working" is advocated for making a good tree. In double-working a scion of a variety such as *Pitmaston Duchess, Beurré d'Amanlis, Fertility* or *Hessle*, which take well on quince, is first budded or grafted on to the quince stock. When this scion has made one season's growth a scion of the incompatible variety is budded or grafted on to this "intermediate" or "first scion." Varieties which are said to do best when double worked, apart from those already mentioned, are *Souvenir, de Congrès, Calebasse Bosc, Beurré Clairgeau, Beurré Rance, Comte de Lamy, Doyenné d'Eté, Jargonelle, Marie Louise, Monarch, Nec Plus Meuris*, and *Thompson's.*

Scion Rooting in Pears on Quince.—When the trees have been planted with the graft or bud union below ground, or when soil has been drawn up to cover the union, the part of the pear stem so covered sometimes forms strong pear roots which compete with the quince roots to such an extent that these often die. When this happens, the tree grows very strongly, with an upright habit of growth, and shows a disinclination to fruit. When such symptoms suggest scion rooting, it is wise to dig the soil away from round the stem, and if young scion roots are seen to be growing out above

THE PEAR

the union, they can be cut off flush with the stem. If there is only one scion root and it is of any size, it is risky to cut it off completely, in case the quince roots have already perished. In this case, the single scion root can be cut off about a foot away from the stem, or alternatively the tree can be bark-ringed (see page 60). When a pear tree on quince is showing the signs of incompatibility between stock and scion mentioned above, and no amount of pruning or manuring will increase its vigour, the balance may be restored either by inarching it with a vigorous seedling pear stock (see page 281) or by inducing the tree to send out scion roots. To do this, the soil should be drawn up to the stem until the union is well covered, and conditions for root growth should be encouraged by mulching the soil round the stem.

PLANTING

Pears, like apples, are best planted in the autumn, but where this is impossible, they may be planted early in spring. Planting should be carried out as in the directions given for apples.

Standards or half-standards on pear stock, unless planted for a shelter belt, should be planted from 18 to 25 feet apart all ways, according to soil and variety. Bush and pyramid trees on quince from 12 to 15 feet apart all ways.

The fuseau can be planted as closely as 6 feet by 3 feet, but a square plant of 6 feet is probably better, and even this is rather close.

Espaliers, and most of the various other forms of wall- or wire-trained trees on pear stock, should be planted at from 15 to 20 feet apart, according to variety and stock, in rows not less than 6 feet apart. Single cordons require 2 feet, double cordons 5 feet, treble cordons (grid-irons) 8 feet in the row.

In the more natural forms, the younger the trees are when planted the better. Bush, pyramid, fuseau and cordon trees should be planted as maidens ; standards or half-standards as two-year-olds. The espaliers and other artificial forms, if bought already trained, are likely to be four or five years old. Those who wish to shape the trees into these forms, should plant maidens and follow the directions in Chapter VI.

PEARS FOR GROWING AS ESPALIERS

Belle Julie	Durondeau	Le Brun
Beurré Six	Emile d'Heyst	Louise Bonne d'Avranches
Conference	Glou Morceau	Marie Louise
Doyenné du Comice	Laxton's Superb	Williams (Bon Chrétien)

THE PEAR

PEARS RECOMMENDED FOR CORDON CULTURE

Belle Julie
Beurré Alexandre Lucas
Beurré Easter
Beurré Six
Beurré Superfin

Conference
Doyenné du Comice
Durondeau
Emile d'Heyst
Marie Louise

Olivier de Serres
Seckle
Thompson's
Triomphe de Vienne
Williams (Bon Chrétien)

PEARS RECOMMENDED FOR BUSH AND PYRAMID FORMS

Belle Julie
Beurré Alexandre Lucas
Beurré Giffard
Beurré Hardy
Beurré Naghin
Beurré Six
Comte de Lamy

Conference
Doyenné d'Eté
Durondeau
Emile d'Heyst
Fondante d'Automne
Laxton's Superb

Le Brun
Louise Bonne d'Avranches
Marguerite Marillat
Souvenir de Congrès
Thompson's
Williams (Bon Chrétien)

PEARS FOR WALL CULTURE

(See page 287.)

PRUNING OF PEARS

Winter Pruning.—In commercial plantations, pears are generally pruned in the winter in the same way as apple trees, the leaders or extension shoots being left uncut, tipped or cut hard back according to the age and vegetative vigour of the tree. The less winter pruning a young tree receives, the sooner it will come into bearing ; when the tree has carried one or two good crops, pruning again becomes necessary to keep up the vegetative vigour of the tree by stimulating fresh shoot growth. Trees which become covered with fruit buds and which set enormous crops will require severe winter pruning.

Trees which grow many strong shoots and produce little blossom should be winter pruned as little as possible until they again come into cropping.

It is generally considered that in winter pruning pear trees, the new lateral side shoots may be cut back or " spurred " fairly drastically without either causing the death of the basal part of the shoots or producing a number of strong new laterals as is too often the case with apples.

Summer Pruning.—Although opinions differ as to the best time for summer pruning pears, it will generally be found that the new green shoots begin to lignify in July, and this is probably the best period at which to cut or brutt them at about the fifth leaf. Leaders, or extension shoots, should never be summer pruned in this way. Lorette pruning in France was concerned mainly with pears, and although the system has been severely criticized in this country, there seems no reason in theory why it should not prove successful in normal seasons, with certain varieties such as *Pitmaston, Beurré Hardy* and *Laxton's Superb*, which make a lot of strong wood-growth. The system depends on stimulating dormant buds at the base of strong new shoots of the current season's growth by cutting those shoots right back to the base when they are beginning to get woody. Lorette fixed more or less arbitrary dates for this under his known climatic conditions at Wagnonville, beginning in May and repeating the process three or four times at intervals of about a month.

Unfortunately it often happens in this country that this short summer pruning does not have the desired effect of stimulating basal fruit-buds, and a whole forest of weak secondary growth springs up. When this happens, the only thing to do is to cut or brutt these secondary growths back and try again the next season.

Lorette advocated pruning each extension shoot or "leader" in the normal way, but he did it late in the spring when the new terminal shoot was already about an inch long. This is probably quite an important part of the Lorette pruning process, and in any case is likely to prevent or weaken the growth of very coarse laterals immediately below the terminal.* (See also page 58.)

PRUNING IN RELATION TO VARIETAL HABIT

Like all fruit trees, pears have marked varietal habits which should be taken into account when pruning or shaping the trees. Upright-growing varieties like *Comice* should have their leaders cut to outside buds, but drooping varieties like *Beurré d'Amanlis* should be pruned to upward buds. Tip-bearing varieties like *Marguerite Marillat* are very difficult to grow as cordons because the fruit is borne at the end of long, slender, twiggy shoots, and if these are "spurred" back, little or no fruit-buds remain on the tree.

PEARS NEEDING HARD PRUNING AT CERTAIN STAGES

Variety	Season	Cooking or Dessert
Beurré Diel	October to November	Dessert
Doyenné d'Eté	July to August	Dessert
Olivier de Serres	February to March	Dessert
Seckle	October to November	Dessert

* The Lorette pruning method was given a thorough trial with apples by the late Mr. A. H. Lees when on the staff at Long Ashton Research Station, and a detailed report of his findings was published in the Annual Report of that station for the year 1920. See also "Lorette Pruning," by Lorette, translated by W. H. Dykes.

THE PEAR

PEARS NEEDING LIGHT PRUNING AT CERTAIN STAGES

Variety	Season	Cooking or Dessert
Bellissime d'Hiver	November to March	Cooking
Beurré Clairgeau	October to November	Cooking
Beurré Hardy	October	Dessert
Clapp's Favourite	August to September	Dessert
Conference	October to November	Dessert
Doyenné du Comice	November	Dessert
Durondeau	October to November	Dessert
Hessle or Hazel	September to October	Dessert
Joséphine de Malines	December to February	Dessert
Marguerite Marillat	September to October	Dessert
Pitmaston Duchess	October to November	Cooking or Dessert

CROSS-POLLINATION

It is generally recognized by fruit-growers to-day that however " self-fertile " a variety of pear may be said to be, it is always wise to plant one or more pollinating varieties within easy flying distance for insects, and to ensure that the flowers of these varieties overlap to a certain extent in their blossoming period.

To plant a single pear tree in a garden or plantation without any other variety of pear from which pollen may be carried to it by insects, is a practice which cannot under any circumstances be recommended. In situations of this kind, where space will not permit of the planting of another tree, the difficulty can usually be got over by top-grafting or frame-working one or more limbs of the solitary tree with scions of another variety with a similar blossoming period. From what has been said above it will be realized that a hive of bees in the vicinity of the garden or plantation is an invaluable aid to cross-pollination. (See tables, page 300.)

MANURING

There is very little experimental evidence as to the manurial requirements of pears, but the most successful pear growers are unanimous in recommending generous dressings of nitrogen and potash, and most of them apply phosphates, also, to be on the safe side. Nothing can beat really good farmyard manure dug in round the trees in winter, or failing that, shoddy, pig-dung or poultry manure, meat and bonemeal, rape dust or castor meal dug in during the winter and supplemented in February or March by 2 cwt. per acre (1 oz. per square yard) of sulphate of potash. In the spring, if the trees set a really heavy crop, some growers like to apply, in addition, a complete application of artificial fer-

17

THE PEAR

tilizers such as would be given for potatoes ; i.e. sulphate of ammonia 1 cwt. per acre (½ oz. per square yard) ; superphosphates 5 cwt. per acre (2½ oz. per square yard) ; sulphate of potash 1 cwt. per acre (½ oz. per square yard).

MULCHING AND WATERING

Trees grown against walls or in very dry situations may find it difficult to hold their crop in a hot summer. Under these conditions a good mulching with some decaying organic matter, such as old compost or lawn mowings, will help to keep moisture in the soil. Before applying the mulch, the ground must be hoed to break any pan that may have formed on the surface.

There are occasions when pear trees on quince carrying a heavy crop of pears, will respond to a good drenching of water, but this should be regarded rather as an emergency measure for wall trees in drought conditions where it is obvious that the tree is wilting for want of moisture. A mulch put on after watering is a great help in preventing rapid evaporation.

THINNING

Fruits should never touch one another on the tree. Each fruit should have ample room to develop.

Varieties bearing small fruit naturally need thinning more drastically than the larger fruiting kinds, which may be allowed to carry two or even three pears on each spur.

PROTECTION FROM BIRDS AND WASPS

Choice individual fruits should be protected whilst still hanging on the tree from the attacks of birds and wasps by means of nets or muslin bags, and if these are tied to the branch or spur, they will prevent the fruit falling and incurring damage.

PEARS FOR WALL CULTURE

Amiral Gervais (South)
Bergamotte d'Esperen (South)
Beurré Diel (South)
Beurré Easter (South)
Beurré Hardy (West)
Beurré Rance (South)
Beurré Superfin (West)
Blickling (West)
Comte de Lamy (South)
Doyenné du Comice (South or West)
Doyenné d'Eté (East)
Emile d'Heyst (West)
Glou Morceau (South or West)
Jargonelle (North, West or N.W.)

Joséphine de Malines (South or West)
Knight's Monarch (South)
Le Lectier (South)
Marie Benoist (South)
Marie Louise d'Uccle (South)
Nec Plus Meuris (South or West)
Nouvelle Fulvie (South)
Olivier de Serres (West)
Passe Crassane (South)
Williams (Bon Chrétien) (North East or East)
   Almost any good Dessert variety will do well on a South Wall.

18

THE PEAR

GATHERING AND STORING

The fruit of the early and mid-season kinds should be gathered before it easily separates from the tree, when gently raised on a level with the stalk, which means that it is ripe. *Williams* must not be yellow when picked or they will quickly go soft. Early fruit intended for market requires very careful selection, handling and packing. It is best sent away as soon as gathered, though some sorts may be stored a few days. Early fruits for private consumption should be laid out singly and allowed to ripen for a few days, being eaten at once, as few of the early varieties keep. The mid-season and late kinds must be stored for a time, as they are not in condition for use when picked. Pears need to be stored at an even temperature of between 40° F. and 45° F. The fruit is best stored in trays in single layers, and not allowed to touch one another. Every care should be taken not to bruise it. The fruit should be inspected from time to time so that any decayed pear may be removed before it contaminates other pears near it. It is not always easy to tell when pears are beginning to ripen. With several varieties, however, the skin becomes a golden yellow, or the tinge of red, if present, will become brighter. Late dessert pears, especially, need care, and should be allowed to hang on the trees as long as possible. Most of the fruit, however, should be gathered before the beginning of November.

Recent investigations suggest the desirability of keeping pears separately from apples in store. It may even be wise to store pears of different seasons separately, varieties of the season of *Beurré Hardy, Conference* and *Doyenné du Comice* being kept away from early varieties like *Williams* and *Laxton's Superb* and from really late-keeping varieties like *Joséphine de Malines, Glou Morceau* and *Winter Nelis*.

Oiled paper wraps should not be used for pears which are to be stored for any length of time.

Before attempting to place pears in gas storage, the advice of the county horticultural officer should be sought as to the varieties which can safely be stored in this way, and as to the temperature and gas concentration required for such varieties. (See also instructions for Gas Storage, page 116.)

MARKETING

Pears are sent to market in much the same manner as apples ; cookers in sieves or bushels, and dessert pears in boxes, half-boxes or trays. (See Apple.)

PEARS—*Doyenné du Comice* (*top*) and *Durondeau* (*bottom*)

F.G.

THE PEAR

INSECT PESTS OF THE PEAR

PEAR APHIS *(Yezabura Pyra)*

This is the only one of the several species of green fly occurring on Pears that does much damage. In appearance and habits it very much resembles the Rosy Apple Aphis (see Apple, page 156), and it is amenable to the same remedies.

COMMON GREEN CAPSID *(Lygus pabulinus)*

Sometimes corky, dimpled patches are found on pear fruits and are caused by the feeding of this Capsid Bug, which is best known as a pest of bush fruits. (See Currants, page 234.)

APPLE BLOSSOM WEEVIL   (See Apple, page 157.)

CATERPILLARS   (See Winter Moths, under Apple, page 155.)

CODLING MOTH *(Cydia pomonella)*

The habits of this pest are much the same on this fruit as they are on apples. On pears there is a greater tendency for the larvæ to enter the eye rather than at the side, making control somewhat easier. Arsenical sprays should be applied late in June or early in July. (See also Apple, page 160.)

PEAR AND CHERRY SLUGWORM *(Caliroa limacina)*

The black slug-like larvæ of this pest occur on pears and cherries in August, and feed on the upper surface of the leaves, eating away the tissue to leave pale brown blotches. Badly-attacked leaves turn brown and fall, and small trees have been known to be almost defoliated as a result. The " slug " is really the young stage of a sawfly and hatches from an egg laid in the leaf tissues. Although green in colour, it exudes a very dark green slime which makes it resemble a black slug. When fully fed it spins a cocoon in the soil (much after the style of the Apple Sawfly larva) wherein it pupates and whence the adult sawfly ultimately emerges the following July.

Control.—This pest, which can be very serious, is, fortunately, easy to destroy. Almost any kind of dry powder such as Derris dust or nicotine dust will get rid of it since it absorbs the slime and dries up the larva.

If preferred, a spray of lead arsenate may be used and is very effective.

T—F.G.

INSECT PESTS OF THE PEAR

PEAR MIDGE (*Diplosis pyrivora*)

In some districts this insect is a very serious pest and considerably reduces the yield of fruit, since fruitlets attacked by it invariably fall off. An attack of this pest is readily diagnosed soon after the fruit has set. Infected fruitlets swell abnormally, often becoming deformed. Within a few weeks they begin to crack and decay and drop off the trees. The centres of such fruits will be found to consist of wet, black debris together with a number of small, white, legless maggots, up to about one-sixth of an inch in length.

These maggots escape when the attacked fruits fall to the ground and burrow into the soil, their curious jumping powers enabling them to travel short distances. They pupate in the soil and emerge as small, inconspicuous midges the following April, ready to lay eggs in the pear blossom.

Control.—This is an extremely difficult pest to deal with. On small trees in gardens the infected fruit can be collected and destroyed. It is little use doing this, however, if the pest is allowed to go unchecked in neighbouring gardens.

In commercial orchards little can be done beyond frequent cultivation in June and July and stocking with poultry in April, May and June.

Some pears suffer to a greater extent than others, e.g., *Williams* are often badly attacked, whilst late-flowering varieties usually escape altogether.

PEAR LEAF BLISTER MITE (*Eriophyes pyri*)

This pest causes pimples or blisters on the young leaves, first noticeable in the spring, which often are reddish in colour. Severely attacked leaves may eventually turn brown and fall. When numerous, the pest attacks the fruitlets, which may die as a result or become deformed.

The animal responsible for the damage is a mite of microscopic dimensions (less than one-hundredth of an inch in length) which spends the winter under the bud scales and comes out in spring to feed on the leaves and fruits. Eggs are laid in the blisters which the mites give rise to and within which the mites feed and multiply during the whole summer. In the autumn they return to the shelter of the bud scales.

Control.—Either lime sulphur or a petroleum-oil spray should be applied to the trees as soon as the leaves have fallen or when the buds open in the spring.

DISEASES AND PESTS OF THE PEAR

MINOR PESTS

Generally speaking, pears are not so prone to attack by the host of minor pests which infect the apple. Occasional cases may be encountered of the Social Pear Sawfly (*Pamphilus flaviventris*), the black and yellow caterpillars of which live in a " tent " much after the fashion of those of the Lackey Moth. Sometimes also an attack of Leaf-curling Midge (*Dasyneura pyri*) may be seen.

DISEASES OF THE PEAR

PEAR SCAB (*Venturia pirina*)

Much of what is written under Apple Scab applies also to Pear Scab, but the two diseases are quite distinct biologically ; that is, the Pear Scab fungus cannot infect apples, and vice versa. The symptoms of the two diseases are similar, but, with Pear Scab, the fruits are usually infected before the leaves, which, until blossom time, are tightly rolled and present very little surface on which spores can alight and cause infections. Infection of young pear shoots, especially of the variety *Fertility*, is often much more severe than with apples, and the individual " pustules " are much larger and more open. They present a ready means of entry for the canker fungus, and indeed areas are known where it is impossible to grow *Fertility* pears unless very efficient spraying for Scab-control is carried out ; they succumb to Canker.

Control.—Unlike most apple varieties, pears can safely be sprayed with Bordeaux Mixture in most seasons. Many pear varieties, however, are injured by lime-sulphur, especially when this is applied post-blossom. To control the disease, a spray should be applied at the same periods of tree development as recommended for Apple Scab, that is, twice before, and at least twice after blossom. Lime-sulphur at 2½ per cent. pre-blossom, followed by Bordeaux Mixture at 4-6-100 post-blossom, or a colloidal copper preparation, is an effective combination, or the copper spray can be used pre- and post-blossom quite satisfactorily. Copper spray is likely to russet the fruits, but this is not a serious blemish in pears, provided the injury is not severe enough to cause cracking of the young fruits. The russeting is more extensive in a wet summer than in a dry one, but it is preferable to the risk of severe leaf-burn and fruit-drop consequent upon the use of lime-sulphur strong enough to be fungicidally effective. The variety *Conference* is highly resistant to Scab in most districts. *Fertility, Comice,* and *Clapp's Favourite* are among the most susceptible.

24

DISEASES AND PESTS OF THE PEAR

BROWN ROTS *(Sclerotinia fructigena and S. laxa)*
(See Plum, page 314.)

CANKER and EYE ROT *(Nectria galligena)*
(See Apple, page 165.)

SOOTY BLOTCH *(Glœodes pomigena)*
(See Plum, page 316.)

ARMILLARIA *(Armillaria mellea)*
(See Apple, page 168.)

BITTER PIT *(Functional)*

This disease appears to be of similar origin to that on apple (see page 173), though some workers now suspect that it may be a virus disease. It differs in appearance from that on apple in that the pits are usually deep so that an affected fruit is dimpled and misshapen. The pits consist of very hard areas that resist the knife when an attempt is made to cut them open, and a badly affected fruit is ruined as a dessert pear.

WATERLOGGING *(Functional)* (See Apple, page 170.)

DISEASES AND PESTS: DIAGNOSIS TABLE
THE PEAR

DAMAGE	PROBABLE CAUSE
Branches and Twigs	*Diseases*
Cankerous formations—patches of small, whitish pustules or crimson spherical bodies grouped together	Canker
Sheets of fungous tissue under bark at base of trunk. Long, black strands like "boot-laces" on roots and in adjacent soil in autumn. Tree dies	Armillaria Root Rot
Shoots and Foliage. (Including Blossom)	*Pests*
Leaves, opening buds and blossom attacked by small "looping," green caterpillars	Winter Moths
Leaves spun together by small, brown, green or yellowish caterpillars, which wriggle quickly backwards when disturbed	Tortrix Moths
Leaves curled and infested by masses of small, bluish-purple aphides. Young shoots twisted, stunted and deformed	Pear Aphis
Flower buds eaten from within in April by black-headed white grub. Blossom remains "capped," turns brown, drops	Apple Blossom Weevil
Leaves torn and distorted, shoots stunted and may be killed	Common Green Capsid Bug
Intervenal tissue of leaves eaten by black, slug-like larvæ in August; leaving pale brown blotches; foliage may turn brown and fall	Pear and Cherry Slugworm
Pimples or blisters on young leaves in spring, often reddish; may turn brown and leaves fall	Pear Leaf Blister Mite
	Diseases
Blister-like "pustules" on shoots and possibly on bud scales in spring. Circular, olive-green spots, turning corky and scab-like later	Pear Scab
Blossom trusses and surrounding foliage of apparently healthy tree wilts about blossom-time	Waterlogging

25

THE PEAR

DISEASES AND PESTS: DIAGNOSIS TABLE (*continued*)

DAMAGE	PROBABLE CAUSE
Fruit	*Pests*
Small fruits eaten by green, "looping" caterpillars	Winter Moth
Maggoty. May drop just before picking-time	Codling Moth
Fruitlets swell abnormally, are deformed, crack, decay and drop—centres, wet black débris and white maggots	Pear Midge
	Diseases
Circular, olive-green spots, velvety at first, turning corky and scab-like in spring and summer	Pear Scab
Brownish, roughly circular, indefinite smudges on skin (usually near picking-time)	Sooty Blotch
Deep pits giving fruits a dimpled appearance; fruits often misshapen; brownish pockets in flesh after picking	Bitter Pit
Brown, soft rot of fruit either on the tree or in store; buff spore pustules or cushions mostly in concentric form	Brown Rot

Note.—Once the trouble has been diagnosed, the reader should refer to the paragraph dealing with the particular disease or pest, and should also consult the Guide to Spraying, see page 144.

VARIETIES OF PEARS

Before deciding which varieties to grow, it is advisable to make a careful study of local conditions, and if possible to find out which varieties are most satisfactory. This is best done by consulting the county advisory officer and local fruit growers.

DESSERT PEARS

Amiral Gervais. A medium-sized, round oval pear, dark russet green ripening to yellowish green. Excellent flavour and good cropper.

André Desportes. A medium-sized, conical pear, pale yellowish-green with reddish-brown flush. Growth moderate; good cropper. May be used to cross-pollinate Doyenné du Comice. Late bloomer; season, August to September.

Belle Julie. A small to medium-sized, oval pear, a russeted golden-brown, flushed red. Of excellent flavour and recommended for garden culture as a cordon, bush, or espalier. Hardy and prolific. Ready for use in October and November. Self-sterile.

Bergamotte d'Esperen. A medium-sized, roundish, flattened, dark green pear, of roughish appearance, turning yellow when ripe. Of delicious flavour. Ready for use from January to March. A choice garden fruit for a warm wall. Said to be self-fertile.

Buerré Alexandre Lucas. A large, roundish, conical fruit, a patchy russeted yellow when ripe. Of juicy and aromatic flavour. Ready November and if gathered before ripe, will store up to January. Recommended for culture as cordon or bush. Self-sterile. Triploid.

Beurré Bachelier. A good quality pear, roundish in shape and green in colour; makes an upright-growing tree of medium vigour and crops well. Season, November to December. Susceptible to scab.

VARIETIES OF DESSERT PEARS

Beurré Bedford. A fine, large, pyriform and tapering pear, of recent introduction. The result of a cross between Marie Louise and Durondeau ; crimson and russet on yellow. Said to be of excellent flavour and a good cropper in all forms. Ready in October. Said to be self-fertile.

Beurré d'Amanlis. A medium to large, round, pyriform, yellowish-green fruit with reddish-brown cheek. Of excellent flavour and a good cropper. Growth very spreading. Hardy and recommended for the Midlands and northern districts. Ready September. Self-sterile. Triploid.

Beurré de Capiaumont. A small to medium-sized, oval, pale yellow, russeted and flushed fruit of medium flavour, and useful for dessert or cooking. Hardy in all forms. Ready October.

Beurré Diel. A very large, roundish, oval, pale green pear turning yellow with russet spots and reddish-brown flush. Of excellent sweet aromatic flavour when grown as bush or pyramid on the quince stock. Ready October to November. Prefers a warm sheltered site and needs a wall in colder districts. Prune hard. Triploid.

Beurré Easter. A medium to large, roundish, oval, yellow-green pear, with russet patches. Of excellent flavour. Hardy and reliable cropper in all forms. Likes a warm, sheltered situation and should be grown against a wall in colder districts. Should be gathered before it is ripe and stored for use from January to February. Prune lightly. Self-sterile.

Beurré Giffard. Medium in size. Yellow with brown flush. Fair flavour. Weak and straggling growth. Very hardy. Ready in August.

Beurré Hardy. A medium, round to conical, brownish, russet-spotted fruit, that does well as an espalier on a west wall on quince stock. Very vigorous grower. Of excellent flavour and should be gathered just before it is ripe. Ready October. Prune lightly. Mid-season flowering. Usually considered a shy cropper. Self-sterile.

Beurré Rance. A large, pyriform, deep green fruit with russet markings. Of fine flavour. Ready for use from December to March. Hardy and prolific, but must have good soil and preferably a position on a south wall. Self-sterile.

Beurré Six. A large, pyriform, light green pear, changing to russety-yellow. Of good flavour. Ready for use in November and December. Hardy and prolific. Self-sterile.

Beurré Superfin. A medium-sized, pyriform, golden-yellow fruit, patched with russet, that thrives on west walls in espalier form. Does well on quince stock and is a fine garden fruit. Prune regularly. Of excellent flavour. Ready October. Requires to be picked early and eaten while still firm. Early flowering and rarely self-fertile.

Blickling. A small, roundish, russety-green pear of very good flavour. Keeping well for use from December to January. Hardy and prolific. Self-sterile.

Bon Chrétien (Williams). A medium-sized to large, pyriform, uneven, pale green fruit turning yellow, with faint red lines and russet spots, when ripe. Of delicious musky flavour. Recommended for garden culture by the Royal Horticultural Society. Does well as a cordon, on a north or east wall, as a half-standard, standard, trained tree, or bush. Ready September. *Should be picked green.* Mid-season flowering and said to be self-fertile. Prune lightly. Should be double worked on quince. (See page 282.)

Calebasse Bosc. A long " calabash-pipe " shaped pear ; dark brown russet. September to October. Superb flavour but most unreliable cropper and very subject to scab. Should be grown as espalier and sprayed carefully. Sometimes wrongly called Beurré Bosc.

Chalk. A small, roundish, light green pear, russeted and flushed. Of poor flavour. Ready early August. A hardy and regular cropper that is frequently planted as a half-standard to act as a screen. The fruit, although of poor flavour, is marketable and should be picked just before it is ripe. Very strong grower with drooping habit. Not a garden fruit.

Charles Ernest. A very large, oval, pyriform, golden-yellow pear, with red flush. Fine rich aromatic flavour. Ready for use in October and November. Hardy and prolific in all forms and does well on quince and pear stock. Good for top-grafting. Self-sterile.

Clapp's Favourite. A medium-sized, pyriform, light yellow fruit with red or bronze cheek, and striped red. Of good flavour. Hardy and prolific in all forms. Ready late August to September and should be picked just before it ripens as it does not keep. A popular market fruit. Late-flowering and said to be self-sterile. Prune lightly.

Comte de Lamy. A small, roundish, greenish-yellow and russeted fruit of delicious flavour. Ready October to November for immediate use. Crops well in all forms but needs a sheltered situation in the warmer counties. A fine wall fruit. Rarely self-fertile.

Conference. A medium-sized to large, pyriform, long-necked, handsome, deep green fruit russeted reddish-brown. Of delicious and aromatic flavour. Ready for picking in late September and a very valuable market pear from October to November. Hardy and a reliable cropper in all forms and on most soils, particularly when grown against a south or west wall. Recommended for garden culture by the Royal Horticultural Society. Said to be self-fertile and a useful pollinator to mix with second-early flowering, self-sterile varieties. *This pear is highly scab resistant.*

Directeur Hardy. A large, pyriform, russeted yellow fruit with flushed cheek. Of fine juicy flavour. Ready from late September to November. Hardy and prolific in all forms. Small tree. Self-sterile.

Dr. Jules Guyot. Large, oval, pyriform, yellow fruit with small black dots and slight flush, very similar to Williams (Bon Chrétien) in appearance. Delicious flavour and a hardy and reliable cropper. A popular market pear, but it must be picked before it ripens as it does not keep long. Ready early in September. Self-fertile. Should be double-worked when on quince. (See page 282.)

Doyenné d'Eté. A small, roundish, yellow fruit, but flushed with reddish-brown, of excellent flavour and ready July to August, but does not store. The earliest pear, but somewhat delicate. Recommended

VARIETIES OF DESSERT PEARS

for cultivation as bush, cordon or espalier against an east wall. Self-sterile. A weak grower. Prune hard. Best on pear stock.

Doyenné du Comice. A medium-sized, oval, pyriform, golden-russet fruit of delicious flavour. Does best as cordon, or espalier against a warm and sheltered south or west wall in a deep brick-earth soil. The best-flavoured market dessert pear. Ready for picking early in October and does not keep long after November in ordinary storage. Recommended for garden culture by the Royal Horticultural Society. Late flowering and self-sterile. Highly susceptible to scab. Pollinators recommended are Glou Morceau, Nouveau Poiteau, Laxton's Superb, Winter Nelis, Beurré Bedford, Clapp's Favourite, André Desportes. One of the most difficult of all pears to induce to crop. Subject to scab.

Durondeau. A large, pyramidal, brown russet fruit flushed red, of good flavour, that is popular at market. Hardy and prolific in all forms and recommended for garden culture. Ready in September, and stores until October and November. Early flowering ; sometimes self-fertile. Prune lightly. Highly susceptible to scab.

Easter Beurré. See Beurré, Easter.

Emile d'Heyst. A medium-sized, long, oval, yellow, russeted pear, of excellent flavour that is ready for picking in September, and is popular at market in October and November. Recommended for garden culture by the Royal Horticultural Society and does well in all forms and in all soils on a pear or quince stock, particularly against a west wall. Hardy and prolific in northern counties. Mid-season flowering. Rarely self-fertile.

Fertility. A small to medium-sized, round-conical, yellow fruit with russet cheek. Of fair flavour. Ready in September and October and does not store. Hardy and prolific in all forms on quince and pear stocks, and even in poor soil. Mid-season flowering. Self-sterile. Highly susceptible to scab and canker. A best seller at seaside markets.

Fondante d'Automne. A medium-sized, roundish, yellow fruit, patched with russet. Of delicious aromatic flavour. Ready in October for immediate use. Hardy and prolific in all forms and in its season one of the best. Self-sterile.

Fondante de Thirriot. A large, conical, clear yellow fruit, with russet spots and rosy-flushed cheek. Of fine flavour. Ready for use in November and December. Hardy and prolific in all forms except standard. Has a very long stalk. Self-sterile.

Glou Morceau. A large, roundish light green to greenish-yellow fruit of rich flavour. Hardy and prolific as espalier on warm south or west wall and in light soil. Late blossomer and a good pollinator for Doyenné du Comice. Ready for picking late October and stores until December or January. Very difficult pear to finish. Self-sterile. A strong grower. Prune regularly.

Hessle or Hazel. A small to medium-sized, roundish, yellow to brownish fruit of fair flavour, and always popular at market. Ready September to October for immediate use. Hardy and prolific in all forms and districts including the north. Self-fertile. Prune lightly.

DESSERT PEARS

Jargonelle. A medium-sized to large, long, conical, greenish-yellow fruit with faint red cheek. Of fine flavour. Hardy and a good bearer in all forms, even in the colder districts of the north. Best when grown as a trained tree on a north, west or north-west wall, but also does well as a standard. Must be picked and eaten straight off the tree. *Will not store.* Early flowering. Prune lightly. Self-sterile. Triploid.

Joséphine de Malines. A small, conical, greenish-yellow pear russeted round the stem. Of delicious flavour and probably the best of the late pears, particularly for market, where it is popular. Hardy and prolific, especially when grown as an espalier against a wall. Recommended for garden culture by the Royal Horticultural Society. Ready early in October and keeps well for use from December to February. Self-sterile. Prune lightly.

Knight's Monarch. A medium-sized, round, conical, russeted, yellow fruit of delicious aromatic flavour. Stores well and ready for use from January to March. Hardy and prolific when grown in the warmer districts. Self-sterile.

Lammas. A small, conical fruit, of second-rate flavour, somewhat similar to Hessle. Ready in August for immediate use. Strong, upright grower. Often grown as a half-standard for shelter. Not a garden fruit.

Laxton's Superb. A fair-sized fruit of good flavour obtained by means of a cross between Beurré Superfin and Williams (Bon Chrétien). Ready August. Hardy and prolific. Precocious cropper. Partially self-fertile.

Le Brun. A long pear, rather like Conference, but with only a small amount of russet. Grows and crops well, but not of first-class flavour. Season, October.

Le Lectier. Medium to large ; greenish-yellow ; strong, upright growth ; cropping moderate. Good flavour, but needs a wall. Season, December to January. Self-sterile.

Louise Bonne d'Avranches (Louise Bonne of Jersey). A medium-sized to large, handsome, conical, yellowish-green pear, with a dark red cheek. Rich flavour. A heavy and regular cropper, especially in the milder districts and in any form. Recommended for garden culture by the Royal Horticultural Society and useful for pot culture. Ready October, but must be picked before it is ripe. Mid-season-flowering. Partially self-fertile.

Marguerite Marillat. A very large, long, uneven-shaped, golden-yellow pear, tinged red and russeted. Of fair flavour. It should be gathered before it is ripe and stored for use in September and October. Recommended for culture as a bush. Hardy and prolific in warm and sheltered positions. Early flowering. Said to be self-fertile. Prune lightly, leaving tip-bearing laterals full length in early years.

Marie Benoist. A large, uneven-shaped pear russeted over yellow ; of fair flavour and a valuable late fruit. Given favourable conditions on a south wall or in a warm, sheltered situation, it is a good cropper, but otherwise results may be very disappointing. Should be gathered late in October and stored for use in February. Self-sterile.

Marie Louise. Long, oval fruit, pale greenish-yellow. Good flavour. Straggling growth and makes many spurs. Season, October to November.

30

DESSERT PEARS

Self-fertile. Makes a small tree ; very suitable for garden culture, but subject to scab.

Marie Louise d'Uccle. A large, pyriform, pale green to yellow fruit with russet patches. Ready October to November. Of delicious flavour. Hardy and prolific in all forms. In colder districts requires wall protection. Should be picked before it is ripe if for market as it does not keep long. A tip-bearer. Subject to scab. Mid-season flowering. Self-fertile.

Moor Fowl's Egg (Muirfowl's Egg). Small to medium-sized, yellowish-green fruit russeted and rosy cheeked. Ready in October. Of fair flavour. A hardy and prolific cropper even in the north and Scotland.

Nec Plus Meuris. A small to medium-sized, greenish-yellow fruit, slightly russeted and of delicious flavour. Stores well, and is ready for use from February to March. Hardy and prolific as bush, cordon, pyramid or espalier. Difficult to ripen in the open, except on wall. Self-fertile.

Nouvelle Fulvie. A medium to large, conical, green fruit, turning yellow, russeted with flushed cheek. Of rich flavour. Stores well and is ready for use from December to February. Hardy and prolific but requires a position on a warm wall in the colder districts. Rarely self-fertile.

Nouveau Poiteau. A large, greenish-yellow pear with reddish russet, and of excellent flavour. Has been recommended as pollinator for Comice. Season, November. Late flowering.

Olivier de Serres. A medium-sized, flattish, round, russeted yellow pear of delicious flavour. Stores well when gathered late and ready for use from February to March. Hardy and prolific in all forms except as a standard, in which form it is unreliable in this country. The shelter of a west wall is desirable. Self-sterile. Prune hard. A very weak grower.

Passe Colmar. A medium-sized, yellow and reddish-brown fruit of good flavour. Ready for use in November and December. Hardy and prolific in all forms. Rarely self-fertile.

Passe Crassane. A large, flattish, round, russeted green fruit of fine flavour. Stores well for use from January to March. Hardy and prolific in favourable conditions in a mild climate and good pear soil. Self-sterile.

Pitmaston Duchess. A very large, long, pyriform, golden-yellow, russeted pear of good flavour for dessert or cooking. Ready for use in October and November, but should be gathered towards the end of September. Hardy and very vigorous in all forms. Too vigorous for small gardens. A popular market and exhibition pear. Late flowering. Partially self-fertile. Prune lightly. A shy cropper in many districts. A triploid and therefore not to be recommended as a pollinator for other varieties.

Princess. A large, handsome, yellow fruit, tinged with red. Of first-rate flavour. Ready for use in November and December. Hardy and prolific in all forms. Self-sterile.

Roosevelt. A very large, roundish, green pear, flushed red. Of fair flavour. Ready about the middle of October and marketed in November. Hardy and prolific in all forms and particularly attractive in blossom. Said to be self-sterile.

Seckle. A small, spotted, brownish-red fruit of honey-like sweetness. Ready for use from October to November. Hardy and prolific in all forms. Rarely self-fertile. Very weak growing.

Souvenir de Congrès. Very large, handsome, pyriform, yellow fruit, russeted and rosy cheeked. Fine flavour. Best when double grafted on quince stock. Ready for use from August to September. Hardy and a good bearer in all forms. Rarely self-fertile.

Thompson's. A medium-sized, uneven-shaped, yellow fruit slightly russeted. Of delicious flavour and crops well as a standard. Ready from October to November. Self-sterile. A good pear, now seldom grown.

Triomphe de Vienne. A medium-sized, conical, russeted, yellow fruit, flushed red. Of good flavour. Ready in September, but best picked before it is ripe. Hardy and prolific in all forms in good pear soil. Rarely self-fertile.

Williams. See Bon Chrétien.

Winter Nelis. A small, dull-green pear, changing to yellow and spotted with black specks. Of delicious flavour and a market favourite. Ready for picking early in October, and stores for use from December to January if gathered before it is ripe. It is hardy and a good cropper if grown in warm and sheltered situations and makes a good wall fruit or espalier. A weak grower. Difficult to ripen. Rarely self-fertile.

COOKING PEARS

Bellissime d'Hiver. A large, yellow fruit with red flush, and of good flavour when cooked. Ready November to March and stores well. Hardy and prolific as a pyramid or standard, and may also be grown as a cordon or bush. Prune lightly. Said to be self-fertile.

Beurré Clairgeau. A large, handsome and remarkably fertile, oval, lemon-yellow to golden-brown fruit, flushed orange and red. Ready from November to December. Hardy and prolific even in the northern counties. Stores well for a short time and is a profitable market pear. Makes a large upright bush or standard on pear stock and needs only light pruning. Said to be self-sterile.

Beurré de Capiaumont. See Dessert Pears.

Beurré Naghin. A medium-sized, round, bright green pear with a long stalk. Medium growth ; good cropper and excellent quality.

Catillac. A large, roundish, dull green pear, tinged reddish-brown and ripening to a deep reddish-brown. Ready to pick in October and stores well. A profitable market fruit from December to April. Recommended for garden culture by the Royal Horticultural Society. Does well as standard, espalier, pyramid, or trained tree on north or east walls. Hardy and prolific, but an uncertain cropper on some soils. Mid-season flowering. Self-sterile. Triploid. Prune lightly. Too vigorous grower for small gardens.

VARIETIES OF PEARS

General Todleben. A very large, greenish-yellow and russeted pear, of exceptional flavour. May be worthy of dessert sometimes. Ready early in October, and stores well into January. Does well in all forms and needs only light pruning. Self-sterile. Difficult to ripen.

Vicar of Winkfield. A large, longish, bright green fruit, turning yellow. Of excellent flavour and may be used for dessert. Ready early in October and storing for use from November to January. Hardy and prolific in all forms. Prune lightly. Triploid.

Many dessert pears, if gathered when they are hard and green, cook splendidly, and when the trees are cropping heavily, it is wise to thin out and cook a quantity, and thus give the remaining fruit more chance to develop into choice specimens. For the small grower the following three varieties make a highly satisfactory combination : **Conference**, **Laxton's Superb** and **Dr. Jules Guyot.** If only one tree is to be selected, it had better be the first of these.

THE CROSS-POLLINATION OF PEAR VARIETIES

When only one pear tree is planted, it is essential to select one of the self-fertile varieties, unless, of course, other pear trees, flowering at the same period, are growing in other gardens close by.

SELF-FERTILE VARIETIES

Early-flowering	Mid-season-flowering	Late Bloomers
Bergamotte d'Esperen Conference Durondeau Marguerite Marillat	Bellissime d'Hiver Beurré Bedford Bon Chrétien (Williams) Marie Louise	Dr. Jules Guyot

PARTIALLY OR SOMETIMES SELF-FERTILE

Early-flowering	Mid-season-flowering	Late Bloomers
Beurré Superfin	Laxton's Superb Louise Bonne of Jersey	Hessle or Hazel Pitmaston Duchess

The John Innes Horticultural Institution have proved that Beurré d'Amanlis cannot be cross-pollinated by Conference, nor Louise Bonne by Conference. Apart from these any of the fertile or partially self-fertile varieties planted in conjunction with self-sterile varieties, flowering at the same time, will cross-pollinate the self-sterile varieties. Early-flowering sorts will also cross-pollinate mid-season flowers and mid-season bloomers cross-pollinate late bloomers, as the flowering seasons overlap somewhat.

VARIETIES OF PEARS

SELF-STERILE AND RARELY SELF-FERTILE VARIETIES

Early-flowering	Mid-season-flowering	Late Bloomers
Beurré d'Amanlis	Catillac	Calebasse Bosc
Beurré Clairgeau	Emile d'Heyst	Clapp's Favourite
Beurré Diel	Joséphine de Malines	Doyenné du Comice
Beurré Hardy	Winter Nelis	Fertility
Comte de Lamy		Glou Morceau
Doyenné d'Eté		Nouveau Poiteau
Jargonelle		Passe Colmar
Souvenir de Congrés		

14 GOOD VARIETIES OF PEAR

Variety	Garden or Orchard	Dessert or Cooking
Beurré Superfin	Garden or Orchard	Cooking or Dessert
Bon Chrétien (Williams)	Garden or Orchard	Dessert
Conference	Garden	Dessert
Doyenné d'Eté	Garden	Dessert
Doyenné du Comice	Garden	Dessert
Durondeau	Garden	Dessert
Emile d'Heyst	Garden or Orchard	Dessert
Glou Morceau	Garden or Orchard	Dessert
Jargonelle	Garden	Dessert
Joséphine de Malines	Garden	Dessert
Laxton's Superb	Garden or Orchard	Dessert
Louise Bonne of Jersey	Garden	Dessert
Pitmaston Duchess	Garden or Orchard	Cooking or Dessert
Winter Nelis	Garden or Orchard	Dessert

PEARS FOR LARGE OR MEDIUM GARDENS

Variety	Dessert or Cooking	Season
Belle Julie	Dessert	October–November
*Bergamotte d'Esperen	Dessert	January–March
Beurré Easter	Dessert	January–February
*Beurré Hardy	Dessert	October
Beurré Six	Dessert	November–December
Beurré Superfin	Dessert	October
*Bon Chrétien (Williams)	Dessert	September
Conference	Dessert	October–November
Doyenne d'Eté	Dessert	July–August
*Doyenné du Comice	Dessert	November
Durondeau	Dessert	October–November
*Emile d'Heyst	Dessert	October–November
*Jargonelle	Dessert	August–September
*Joséphine de Malines	Dessert	December–February
Laxton's Superb	Dessert	August–September
*Louise Bonne of Jersey	Dessert	October
*Olivier de Serres	Dessert	February–April
Seckle	Dessert	October–November
Vicar of Winkfield	Cooking	November–January
*Winter Nelis	Dessert	December–March

* Recommended for Wall.

34

VARIETIES OF PEARS

SELECTION OF PEARS IN ORDER OF RIPENING
Early (August–September)

Variety	Garden or Orchard	Dessert or Cooking
Bon Chrétien (Williams)	Garden or Orchard	Dessert
Clapp's Favourite	Garden or Orchard	Dessert
Doyenné d'Eté	Garden	Dessert
Dr. Jules Guyot	Garden or Orchard	Dessert
Hessle	Garden or Orchard	Dessert
Jargonelle	Garden	Dessert
Laxton's Superb	Garden or Orchard	Dessert
Souvenir de Congrés	Garden	Dessert

Mid-Season (October–November)

Variety	Garden or Orchard	Dessert or Cooking
Beurré Clairgeau	Garden or Orchard	Dessert or Cooking
Beurré d'Amanlis	Garden	Dessert
Beurré Diel	Garden	Dessert
Beurré Hardy	Garden or Orchard	Dessert
Beurré Superfin	Garden	Dessert
Conference	Garden or Orchard	Dessert
Doyenné du Comice	Garden	Dessert
Durondeau	Garden	Dessert
Emile d'Heyst	Garden	Dessert
Fondante d'Automne	Garden	Dessert
Louise Bonne of Jersey	Garden	Dessert
Marguerite Marillat	Garden	Dessert
Marie Louise	Garden	Dessert
Marie Louise d'Uccle	Garden	Dessert
Pitmaston Duchess	Orchard	Cooking or Dessert

Late Season (November–December, etc.)

Variety	Garden or Orchard	Dessert or Cooking
Beurré Alexandre Lucas	Garden or Orchard	Dessert
Beurré Easter	Garden or Orchard	Dessert
Beurré Naghin	Garden or Orchard	Cooking
Beurré Rance	Garden or Orchard	Dessert
Catillac	Garden or Orchard	Cooking
Glou Morceau	Garden or Orchard	Dessert
Joséphine des Malines	Garden	Dessert
Passe Colmar	Garden	Dessert
Nec Plus Meuris	Garden or Orchard	Dessert
Vicar of Winkfield	Garden or Orchard	Cooking
Winter Nelis	Garden or Orchard	Dessert

PEARS FOR FORCING

Variety	Season	Dessert or Cooking
Beurré Hardy	October	Dessert
Beurré Superfin	October–November	Dessert
Doyenné du Comice	October–November	Dessert
Louise Bonne of Jersey	October	Dessert

35

VARIETIES OF PEARS

SOME GOOD-FLAVOURED DESSERT PEARS

Variety	Garden or Orchard	Season
Beurré Superfin	Garden	October
Beurré Hardy	Garden or Orchard	October
Bon Chrétien (Williams)	Garden	September
Calebasse Bosc	Garden	September–October
Comte de Lamy	Garden	October–November
Doyenné du Comice	Garden	November
Joséphine de Malines	Garden	December–February
Marie Louise	Garden	October–November
Olivier de Serres	Garden	February–March
Seckle	Garden	October–November
Thompson's	Garden	October–November
Winter Nelis	Garden or Orchard	December–March

SOME PEARS FOR MARKET

Variety	Season	Dessert or Cooking
*Beurré Clairgeau	October–November	Cooking or Dessert
Beurré d'Amanlis	September	Dessert
*Catillac	December–April	Cooking
*Clapp's Favourite	August–September	Dessert
*Conference	October–November	Dessert
Dr. Jules Guyot	September (Early)	Dessert
Doyenné du Comice	November	Dessert
*Durondeau	October–November	Dessert
*Emile d'Heyst	October–November	Dessert
*Fertility	September–October	Dessert
Fondante de Thirriot	November–December	Dessert
*Hessle or Hazel	September–October	Dessert
*Joséphine de Malines	December–February	Dessert
Laxton's Superb	October	Dessert
Louise Bonne of Jersey	October	Dessert
Marie Louise	October–November	Dessert
*Pitmaston Duchess	October–November	Cooking or Dessert
*Roosevelt	November	Dessert

* Varieties suitable for orchard cultivation as standards.

ESPECIALLY HARDY PEARS

Variety	Garden or Orchard	Dessert or Cooking
Beurré Hardy	Garden or Orchard	Dessert
Beurré Superfin	Garden or Orchard	Dessert
Catillac	Garden or Orchard	Cooking
Chalk	Orchard	Dessert
Conference	Garden or Orchard	Dessert
Emile d'Heyst	Garden or Orchard	Dessert
Hessle or Hazel	Garden or Orchard	Dessert
Jargonelle	Garden	Dessert
Louise Bonne of Jersey	Garden or Orchard	Dessert
Lammas	Orchard	Dessert
Pitmaston Duchess	Garden or Orchard	Dessert or Cooking

PEARS FOR GROWING IN POTS (See page 367)

VARIETIES OF PEARS

PEARS FOR STORING

Variety	Gather	Ready for Use
Bergamotte d'Esperen	October	January–March
Beurré Alexandre Lucas	October (before ripe)	November–January
Beurré Clairgeau (C)	Late September	November
Beurré Easter	October	January–February
Beurré Naghin	October	January–March
Blickling	October	December–January
Catillac (C)	Early October	December–April
Conference	Late September	October–November
Doyenné du Comice	Early October	November
Durondeau	Late September	October–November
Emile d'Heyst	Late September	October-November
General Todleben (C)	October	December–January
Joséphine de Malines	Early October	December–February
Marie Benoist	Early October	February
Nec Plus Meuris	October	February–March
Nouvelle Fulvie	October	December–February
Olivier de Serres	October–November	February–March
Passe Crassane	October	January–March
Pitmaston Duchess	Late September	October–November
Roosevelt	Mid-October	November
Vicar of Winkfield (C)	Early October	November–January
Winter Nelis	Early October	December–March

(C) Denotes Cooking.

PEARS FOR EXHIBITION

Variety	Season	Dessert or Cooking
Beurré Bachelier	November–December	Dessert
Beurré Clairgeau	November–December	Cooking
Beurré Hardy	October	Dessert
Beurré Naghin	December–April	Cooking
Catillac	December–April	Cooking
Charles Ernest	October–November	Dessert
Conference	October–November	Dessert
Doyenné du Comice	November–December	Dessert
Marguerite Marillat	October	Dessert or Cooking
Pitmaston Duchess	October–November	Dessert or Cooking

PERRY PEARS

Advice on the best varieties of perry pear to suit the district should first be sought from the County Advisory Officer or Long Ashton.

Perry pears are not now much grown in Devonshire and Somersetshire, but in Herefordshire, Gloucestershire and the Midland cider districts, they are much in demand. They are usually grown as standard trees on seedling pear stocks. Among the best varieties are :—

Barland. A favourite perry pear with a peculiar flavour of its own.

Butt. A medium-sized, conical, green fruit which makes a strong, rough perry. Mid-season to late in flowering. Hardy and prolific. Fruit ready mid-season.

Moorcroft (Malvern Hills). A large, rosy-cheeked, orange and russeted fruit which makes a strong perry. Flowers early to mid-season. Fruit ready late September to early October.

PEARS

There is no tree among all those planted which abounds so much in kinds of fruit as the pear tree, whose different sorts are innumerable and their different qualities wonderful.

DE SERRES, 'THEATRE D'AGRICOLE', 1608

TRACES of the pear have been found in the Swiss lake dwellings of the late Stone Age. Theophrastus, the 'Father of Botany', writing in the third century B.C., mentions several specific kinds, distinguishing between wild and cultivated varieties, and Cato the Elder (235–150 B.C.), who wrote the first book in Latin on agriculture, describes six varieties of pear.

The Romans, and subsequently the Normans, introduced a number of different sorts of pears to this country. Pears are mentioned by both Chaucer and Shakespeare.

By the beginning of the nineteenth century the number of pear varieties had increased very considerably. In 1826 the catalogue of the Royal Horticultural Society enumerated 622 varieties.

Enthusiasm for pear growing was not, however, confined to Britain. During the first half of the nineteenth century, Belgium experienced a tremendous wave of enthusiasm for pear breeding, similar to the Dutch tulip 'mania' three hundred years earlier. The Belgian enthusiasm resulted in the production of such well-known pears as Joséphine de Malines, Marie Louise and Winter Nelis, varieties which are still among the best in cultivation today.

Pear trees are exceptionally long lived, possibly longer than any other fruit save the mulberry. They tend to prefer a slightly warmer soil than apples. Thus pears grow well in the south of France and some of our finest sorts such as Doyenné du Comice, hail from there. In Britain they also fare better in the south.

STOCKS

Quince A can be likened to Malling II. Certain varieties, including the well-known Williams' Bon Chrétien, do not make a good union on quince and such sorts are 'double-worked', that is, a strong growing variety like Beurré Hardy is used as an intermediate direct on to the stock. Quince C can be compared to Malling IX. Pears generally take longer to come into bearing than apples.

SHAPES

Pears do well as bushes or pyramids. They are of more upright growth than apples. Pears are excellent as cordons, espaliers and fan-shaped trees, since they spur readily and are easier to train than apples. Tip-bearing varieties such as Jargonelle and Joséphine de Malines are not suitable for cordons or espaliers. The best flavoured pears are usually those grown alongside sunny walls, due to the radiation of heat finishing the fruits.

CULTIVATION

Pears are happy on most soils, save cold, wet clays, though late varieties such as Glou Morceau, Joséphine de Malines and Winter Nelis are best grown against walls.

Plant 12–15 ft apart as for apples. Great care must be taken to avoid covering the graft or union by planting too deeply, otherwise there is a serious risk of scion rooting, resulting in unmanageable growth and a reluctance to fruit.

Pears require less potash than apples, but enjoy rather more nitrogen. A dressing of sulphate of ammonia or 'Nitro-Chalk' may be given in February or March. Bulky manures such as farmyard manure or compost definitely encourage regular cropping.

Pears will generally tolerate fairly severe pruning. In early winter laterals may be cut back to four or five buds and leaders reduced by one-third. In late July pears may be summer pruned, and this is particularly necessary with cordons and espaliers. Laterals can be reduced to the fifth or sixth leaf from the base—

leaders must only be pruned in winter. Tip-bearing varieties, such as Jargonelle and Joséphine de Malines, should be pruned as for tip-bearing apples like Bramley's Seedling—*see* page 21.

HOW TO PICK PEARS

Unlike apples, pears must not be ripened on the tree or they will turn 'sleepy'. Early and mid-season varieties should be gathered before the green turns to yellow. Care is needed to avoid any bruising, as once pears are bruised, decay sets in. Ripe fruits must be eaten at once or they will deteriorate. Since pears ripen unevenly, they need to be watched very closely. Pears are fit to eat when the flesh round the stem yields to slight pressure of the thumb or finger.

PEARS—CHOICE OF VARIETIES

The division between dessert and culinary pears is less rigid than with dessert and cooking apples. Most pears, if picked when green, cook satisfactorily. Doyenné du Comice, the aristocrat of dessert varieties, is excellent when cooked.

If there is room for only one pear, Conference should be chosen, as it is not only of good flavour but easy to grow, and resistant to the effects of late spring frosts. Conference should be picked in late September and may be eaten from early October to the end of November. In addition to being self-fertile, it is a good pollinator for other varieties.

BEURRE D'AMANLIS

Should be picked at the end of August and is in season about mid-September. Excellent flavour and good cropper. Very hardy and does well in the north and Scotland. Self-sterile, needing two pollinators, e.g. Beurré Bedford, Durondeau, Williams' Bon Chrétien—Conference is unsuitable.

BEURRE HARDY

Should be picked in late September *before* it comes away easily from the stalk. In season from October to December. Excellent flavour. Inclined to make a large tree, but crops regularly when established.

Pollinators: Doyenné du Comice, Laxton's Superb.

BEURRE SUPERFIN

Some people consider this equal in flavour to Doyenné du Comice. Should be picked about mid-September *before* it comes away easily from the stalk.

Pollinators: Conference, Williams' Bon Chrétien.

DOYENNE DU COMICE

The counterpart in pears of Cox's Orange Pippin. Flavour outstanding. Pick at the beginning of October and it will be ready to eat a few weeks later. The fruits should be wrapped in special oiled papers to ensure perfect specimens. Not an easy variety to grow, as it crops irregularly and is probably best against a wall. Successful on heavy soils.

Pollinators: Glou Morceau, Laxton's Superb (the best pollinator), Winter Nelis.

LAXTON'S SUPERB

A cross between Beurré Superfin and Williams' Bon Chrétien. This is probably the finest flavoured early pear and is a heavy cropper. Ready to pick at the end of August—gather just before the fruits are fully ripe—but does not keep and must be eaten soon after picking. A good variety for bottling.

Pollinators: Beurré Hardy, Doyenné du Comice.

MARIE LOUISE

Ready to pick about the end of September and remains good eating for another month.

Pollinators: Beurré Hardy, Laxton's Superb.

WILLIAMS' BON CHRETIEN

A very popular old variety raised as far back as 1770 and of English origin. Should be gathered at the end of August while still green and allowed to ripen naturally. It is ready to eat a few weeks later but does not usually last into October. Though very

sweet and juicy, it has a musky taste which does not appeal to everyone. Needs double working. Very liable to Pear Scab.
Pollinators: Beurré Superfin, Conference.

WINTER NELIS
A small pear of delicious flavour. Should be gathered about the middle of October. May be eaten from early November to late January, and sometimes later, as the fruits ripen rather slowly. Best against a wall, save in sheltered districts. Does not usually succeed on cold soils.
Pollinators: Beurré Hardy, Doyenné du Comice.

PESTS OF THE PEAR
Various aphids and Winter Moths attack pears in the same way as apples, control measures being identical.

PEAR MIDGE (*Contarinia pyrivora* Riley)
Symptoms: Eggs are laid in mid-April inside the pear flowers. The maggot takes about six weeks to mature. Infested fruits grow abnormally large, start to decay and finally fall to the ground. In the blackened centres of the fruits will be found the white, legless maggots of the Midge. When infected fruits drop to the ground, the maggots escape and pupate in the soil, remaining there over the winter. The following April they again emerge as Midges.
Control: Infested fruits should be destroyed. Dr. Massee recommends spraying the surface of the soil with a tar-oil or DNC petroleum wash between bud-burst and white-bud stage, at the rate of approximately one gallon to four square yards. It is essential to use a low pressure to avoid the spray drifting on to the trees themselves, or buds and foliage may be injured. Frequent cultivation round trees in June and July also helps.
COLOURED ILLUSTRATION PAGE 69

PEAR PSYLLID OR SUCKER (*Psyllia pyricola* Först.)
The damage caused by this pest is very similar to Apple Sucker and is also controlled by tar-oil spraying.

PEAR AND CHERRY SLUGWORM (*syn.* PEAR AND CHERRY SAWFLY)
(*Caliroa limacina* Retz.)

Symptoms: The whitish-yellow caterpillars, which subsequently turn black, appear in late June and feed on the upper surface of the leaves, so that they are often partially skeletonized.

Control: Spray or dust with derris or nicotine directly the caterpillars are observed.

DISEASES OF THE PEAR

BROWN ROT (*Sclerotinia fructigena* Aderh. and Ruhl.)

The familiar Brown Rot fungus attacking apples and plums is also found on pears. For control measures, *see* under Apples, page 42.

PEAR CANKER (*Nectria galligena* Bres.)

Apple and Pear Canker are identical diseases, both caused by the same fungus. For control measures, *see* under Apple Canker, page 42. The variety Marie Louise is very susceptible.

PEAR SCAB (*Venturia pirina* Aderh.)

This disease is very similar to Apple Scab. For symptoms and control, *see* under Apple Scab, page 43. Canker attacks generally follow on Pear Scab if the latter is not checked. Doyenné du Comice and Williams' Bon Chrétien are particularly liable to infection, while Conference is usually considered fairly resistant.

DESSERT AND COOKING PEARS

THERE is no doubt that the pear is indigenous to Great Britain. It may still be found growing wild in some parts of the country, though in its wild state the fruits are of little value. It is undoubtedly one of the most delicious fruits to grow in the garden, but one of the most ticklish to tackle. Great care and attention have to be paid to pears if the best results are to be achieved. Garden conditions and climate can have a remarkable effect on the fruit. Pears always seem to do well in the vicinity of running water. The belt of pears along the Medway in Kent is typical of this.

SOIL AND SITUATION

Pears do not like badly drained clay soils nor do they care for light soils that dry out quickly or shallow soils over chalk or gravel. They will grow on most good garden soils with the exception of the later varieties which usually only do well in the South of England. The soil which is supposed to be the ideal is the brick earth of a medium type and one which is not only deep but well drained.

Late keeping pears have to be grown under the most perfect conditions and these include sunny sheltered places and a dry ripening season in the autumn. For this reason in the North most of the late varieties of pears are grown in cool greenhouses. Some of the simpler pears like Conference, Williams and Laxton's Superb do quite well even in the North of England, while the commoner pears like Hessle and Fertility will do well almost anywhere.

Never try and plant pears on a north wall with the

exception, perhaps, of a cooking variety like Uvedale St. Germain. All pear trees against walls will need protection from frost in the spring and ordinary fish netting will do this work well.

TREES TO BUY

As pears need more sunshine on the whole than apples and as on the whole they are slower in coming into bearing it is quite a good plan to purchase pear trees as cordons, as fuseaux, and as pyramids. Bush trees do quite well, especially if the branches are well spaced, and spur pruning is carried out. Cordons however are easy to look after and as more cordons can be planted than any other type, owing to the little room they take up, those with small gardens will probably prefer them.

ROOT STOCKS

It is most important to buy trees guaranteed grafted on the right stocks and then having purchased them to see that the trees are planted shallowly. When trees are planted deeply there is always the danger that the variety of pear will send out roots and so mask or ruin the effect the stock should have. Take for example a Williams grafted on a Quince A stock. If you plant the tree deeply, then roots will grow out from the Williams wood and ruin the effect of the Quince roots which should be controlling the life of the tree. No pear tree, therefore should be planted deeper than, say, 8 inches.

Probably the best stock for the cordons is the Quince C. This is very dwarfing in its effect and trees grafted on it come into cropping quickly. The Quince A is the best stock for the bush, fuseau, or pyramid type of tree, or even for espaliers.

Unfortunately some varieties of pears are incompatible when grafted on to Quince stocks. In these cases it is necessary to graft the trees first of all with another variety and then to graft this variety with the incompatible one. This, of course, is the problem of the nurseryman rather than the purchaser, but the information is given here so that the gardener may know that some of the pear trees have to be double-worked as it is called, and the nurseryman may expect to be paid a little more for a tree which has to be raised in this way.

The younger the trees are when planted the better. Always put in two year olds or one year olds. Bush and pyramid trees need to be 12 ft. square, while fuseau can be 6 ft. by 3ft. Single cordons should be planted 2 ft. apart and be trained at an angle of 45 degrees against the wires.

PRUNING HINTS

As a general rule the side shoots or lateral growths should be cut back to within two or three buds of their base, and this will help to produce fruit buds. The leaders or end growths will be cut back by about half to just above an outward pointing bud, or in the case of branches that are tending to spread, to just above an inward pointing bud.

During the first three or four years it may be necessary to cut the leaders somewhat harder in order to produce strong branches and the side growths could be left alone. It must be remembered that the general rule is, the less winter pruning a young tree receives, the sooner it will come into bearing. Once, however, a tree has started to crop heavily, it is usually necessary to prune the leaders fairly hard so as to ensure that the tree grows well.

When pear trees are old they often become covered with fruit buds and in this case it is usually necessary to thin these out. In bad cases every other spur can be cut out completely. Where such drastic treatment is not thought necessary, the spur could be shortened back so as to remove a number of the fruit buds. A tree will only set a certain amount of blossom satisfactorily and it is foolish to allow a tree to produce very many more flowers than are required.

In the summer it is a good plan to cut back the side growths or laterals to within 2 inches or so of their base as soon as the growths get woody, that is when they are about 8 inches long. This usually means starting summer pruning early in June and continuing once a month until September. Those who do not wish this continuous form of summer pruning should just cut back all the side growth to about the fifth leaf in July.

Some varieties of pears are tip bearers, *e.g.*, Jargonelle and in this case to prune back the laterals is, of course, a mistake. Gardeners should watch the habits of the tree when pruning and work accordingly.

MANURIAL HINTS

Every winter dig in shallowly around the trees farmyard manure or well-rotted composted vegetable refuse at the rate of half a bucketful to the square yard. In January give sulphate of potash at 1 ounce to the square yard and if the trees set a heavy crop in the Spring, give in addition sulphate of ammonia at $\frac{1}{2}$ ounce to the square yard, plus superphosphate at 2 ounces to the square yard. Where composted vegetable refuse or farmyard manure are not obtainable, hop manure or wool shoddy manure may be used instead.

POLLINATION HINTS

Do not forget that a large number of pears are self-sterile. They will not produce friut with their own pollen. See, therefore, that varieties are planted nearby which will produce the right blossom at the right time. Under the heading of Varieties, self-fertile varieties will be found, and all the rest may be said to be self-sterile. There is much to be said for only planting self-fertile varieties in the small garden.

Routine Work

Much of the routine work is concerned with watering and mulching. Wall trees, for instance, often suffer from lack of water in a dry summer time. A good mulching with lawn mowings or similar material in the early summer will do much to keep a heavy crop of pears going.

NOVEMBER
Get all the pruning done and the prunings burnt.

DECEMBER
Spray the trees with a good tar distillate wash.

JANUARY
Apply the farmyard manure, compost vegetable refuse, and dig in shallowly. Apply the sulphate of potash.

APRIL
Get ready to spray the trees just before the blossom opens, with lime-sulphur to keep down Scab. If a heavy crop sets give the sulphate of ammonia and superphosphate.

MAY
Spray again with lime-sulphur directly after all the blossoms have fallen, as the second Scab Spray.
Start carrying out the continuous summer pruning method.

JUNE
Apply a mulching of decaying organic matter around the trees, especially those growing against walls. In very dry weather a good flooding with water may be necessary.
Thin out the pears if a heavy crop has set. Leave no fruit closer than 6 inches apart.

JULY
Carry out the ordinary summer pruning if the continuous method has not been adopted. Put bags on fruits to keep away wasps.

AUGUST-SEPTEMBER
Picking early varieties.

OCTOBER
Continue picking.

Special Hints on Routine Work

(a) Thinning. Tend to thin the varieties which usually carry small fruits more drastically than those which bear large fruits. A variety like Fertility, for instance, generally needs severe thinning while a variety like Pitmaston Duchess which produces a large pear, seldom needs thinning.

(b) Wasp Protectors. Paper bags, butter muslin bags, or net bags can all be used popped over the fruits and tied to the spurs to prevent birds and wasps from damaging the fruits as they are ripening. They also stop the fruits from dropping to the ground.

(c) Picking. Gather the early and mid-season varieties when the stock comes easily away from the spur. Some varieties like Williams should be picked before they are yellow for they go soft so quickly. Later varieties can be stored as advised for apples. If possible always keep pears in separate store from apples for one seems to affect the other. Wrap pears in plain paper not in oiled paper wraps. Pears keep best when stored at a temperature of between 40-45 degrees F. where there is plenty of air, plus darkness. Do not store in too dry a place or the fruit will shrivel.

VARIETIES
SELF-FERTILES

EARLY FLOWERERS	MID-SEASON FLOWERERS	LATE FLOWERERS
Conference	Fertility	Hessle
Durrondeau	Marie Louise	Dr. Jules Guyot
Jargonelle	Williams	Pitmaston Duchess
Margaret Marillat	Buerré Bedford	
Bergamotte	Bellissime d'Hiver	
D'Esperen	Laxton's Superb	

AUGUST-SEPTEMBER PEARS

Williams	Dr. Jules Guyot	Jargonelle
Hessle	Laxton's Superb	Souvenir de Congres

OCTOBER-NOVEMBER PEARS

Conference	Doyenne du Comice	Durrondeau
Margaret Marillat	Marie Louise	Pitmaston Duchess

NOVEMBER-DECEMBER PEARS

Glou Morceau	Josephine de Malines	Winter Nelis
Passe Colmar	Beurré Easter	Beurré Rance

THREE BEST PEARS FOR SMALL GARDEN

Conference	Laxton's Superb	Dr. Jules Guyot

COOKING PEARS

Catillac	Uvedale St. Germain	Vicar of Wakefield

BEST FLAVOURED PEARS

Williams, Sept.	Marie Louise, Oct.	Doyenne du Comice, Nov.
Winter Nelis, Dec.	Thompson's, Oct.-Nov.	Comte de Lamy, Oct.-Nov.

PESTS AND DISEASES. *Practical Points.*

Maggots in Pears. May be caused by either the Codlin Moth, and in this case the larvæ enter the eye and ruin the fruit as in apples, or the Pear Midge, which gets into the fruits as soon as they have set and cause them to swell abnormally. Their centres will be found to consist of black rotten material together with numerous white legless maggots. Answer: In the case of the Codlin Moth, spray with arsenate of lead late in June or early in July. In the case of the Pear Midge, run poultry under the trees in April, May and June; hoe the ground regularly in June and July and pick off all infected fruit immediately it is seen.

Slug Worm. A little pest which looks like a slug, found on the upper surface of the leaves, eating away the tissue. Answer: Dust the trees thoroughly with Derris Dust.

Blister Mite. Blisters or pimples will be found on the young leaves in the spring. Usually red in colour. Sometimes the fruits will be attacked. Answer: Spray with lime-sulphur immediately the leaves have fallen to kill the insect which spends the winter under the bud scales.

Scab. Similar to the Apple Scab, which please see on page 47. Causes black spots on leaves and fruits and in bad cases will cause fruits to crack and be ruined. Young pear wood can also be affected and produce scabby wood. Answer: Spray with lime-sulphur just before the blossoms open, 1 pint to 30 pints water. Spray again with this brown liquid, 1 pint to 60 pints water, immediately all the blossoms have fallen.

PEARS

THE PEAR on the whole grows better in the South of England than in the North though it always succeeds fairly well near rivers where the temperature is equable and where there are no early frosts. Grown in gardens especially against walls it can be given all the protection it needs at blossoming time, even in the North, and so regular cropping may be assured.

SOIL

The pear prefers the well-drained medium loam. It dislikes shallow soil over gravel or chalk and a badly drained clay.

It likes a sheltered and sunny situation and a dry warm, ripening season. For this reason the later ripening sorts of pears seldom do well north of the Thames.

Pears need protection from the East and

North, and should not be planted against a North wall.

BEST TYPES TO GROW

On the whole, pears are slower in coming into bearing than apples. They like the maximum amount of sun. In gardens they may be conveniently grown as bushes, cordons, dwarf pyramids, or trained espaliers. Pears as standards should only be planted in large orchards.

Cordons are particularly suitable, for pears spur readily and are easy to pick and protect when grown in this way.

CORRECT STOCKS

It is most important to purchase trees on guaranteed named stocks. See Chapter 3.

Because it makes for a small tree and immediate cropping most gardeners prefer the Quince C. For bush trees or espaliers, the Quince A stock will do.

Again it is necessary to emphasize that pears must not be planted deeply so as to bury the union of the scion (or variety) and the stock (or root system).

PRUNING

On the whole the same rules of pruning apply to pears as to apples (See Chapter 5).

If it is pruned too hard in its young years, cropping is delayed. When, however, two good crops have been produced, it is necessary to prune fairly hard once more so as to encourage new shoot growth. After many years pears are apt to become covered with hundreds of fruit buds and these must be thinned out. Trees which carry an overdose of blossom seldom set it satisfactorily.

On the whole, harder lateral pruning may be carried out with pears than with apples.

As in the case of apples, some varieties are spreading in their growth, and others upright. They should therefore be pruned accordingly, the upright varieties having the leaders cut to buds pointing outwards and the spreading varieties vice versa.

Typical upright varieties are Comice and Conference. Typical spreaders are Beurre D'Amanlis and Durondeau.

SUMMER PRUNING

This may be carried out with great success as advised for apples.

There is sometimes a difficulty with Pitmaston, Laxton's Superb and Beurre Hardy which tend to make tremendous wood growth, but even with these varieties, if summer pruning is persisted with, ample fruit buds are produced.

MANURES

Pears appreciate organic manure and this in the form of farmyard manure, hop manure, or strawy poultry manure may be dug in around the trees in November and December. In February sulphate of potash should be applied at 1 ounce to the sq. yard or wood ashes at ½ lb. to the sq. yard. In the Spring if it is seen that the trees have set a heavy crop, a complete artificial manure with an organic base, such as Cornish Fish Manure, may be added at 4 ounces to the sq. yard. all around the trees as far as the branches spread.

SPACING AND THINNING

Pears should never be allowed to touch one another. Thinning or spacing should be carried out when the fruits are about the size of a walnut. For further details see Chapter 2.

PICKING

The earlier varieties should be gathered directly the fruits come away from the spurs when lifted in the palm of the hand. The later keeping varieties may be allowed to hang on the trees until the end of October. They should then be picked carefully as advised for apples (See Chapter 5) and may be stored in a similar manner.

It is interesting to note that research has shown the importance of keeping pears in a different store to apples. If this is done they store better, and longer, and are richer flavoured.

VARIETIES

There are hundreds of varieties to choose from but only those are listed which are less particular in their requirements than others.

5

Almost all kinds of pears are eaters, the only important cookers being Catillac and Uvesdale's St. Germain.

SHORT LIST FOR SMALL GARDEN

Laxton's Superb	Williams bon Chretien
Dr. Jules Guyot	Conference
Marie Louise	Durrondeau
Josephine de Malines	

GOOD CORDON PEARS

Conference	Doyenne du Comice
Beurre Ernest	Emile D'Heyst
Glou Morceau	Laxton's Superb
Marie Louise	Williams bon Chretien

BEST BUSH PEARS

Beurre Alexandre Lucas	Conference
Durrondeau	Emile D'Heyst
Laxton's Superb	Margaret Marillat
Thompson's	Williams bon Chretien

PRINCIPAL SELF-STERILE VARIETIES

Beurre Damanlis (E.F.)	Buerre Diel (E.F.)
Doyenne D'ete (E.F.)	Souvenierde Congress (E.F.)

Catillac (M.F.)   Clapp's Favourite (M.F.)
Emile d'Heyst (M.F.) Josephine de Malines
                                             (M.F.)
Doyenne du Qomice (L.F.) Glou Morceau (L.F.)
Beurre Bosc (L.F.)

E.F.—Early Flowering.   M.F. Mid-Season.
L.F.—Late Flowering.

KEEPING PEARS

Winter Nelis   Vicar of Winkfield
                                               (cooker)
Josephine de Malines   Emile D'Heyst
Doyenne du Comice   Conference
Catillac (cooker)   Beurre Easter
Beurre Alexandre Lucas

Pick in October and use as specimens ripen in store.

THE HARDIEST PEARS

Conference   Emile D'Heyst
Hessle   Jargonelle
Louis bon de Jersey   Pitmaston Duchess

SPRAYING PROGRAMME

Month	*What to do*
October ..	Put on grease bands to prevent winter moth caterpillars.
December ..	Spray with tar distillate wash, 5%. Clean tree. Kill aphid eggs.
Early April ..	Spray with lime-sulphur ¼ pt. to 10 pts. water. To prevent Scab and Blister Mite.
	Include little arsenate of lead in wash to kill caterpillars.
April ..	Spray with lime-sulphur as above just before blossoms open. Include little lead arsenate paste again
Mid-May ..	When all petals have fallen dust with copper-lime dust to prevent Scab.
June ..	Dust again with copper lime dust to prevent Scab. Spray with lead arsenate, ¼ lb. lead arsenate paste to 6 galls. water, to kill slug worms and codlin caterpillars.
July	Spray with nicotine or liquid Derris I.T.P. to kill slug worms.

PEARS.

The Pear is said to be the *Prince* of fruits, because of its delicacy, juiciness and rich melting flesh. In this work, written for the plain public, we have classed the apple as *King*.

Our selection of varieties, will by many be ignored, yet we feel that when we name a variety to be grown, we do so knowingly of its past-time value, and hence the probability of its future. Willing to give credit to those who have aided in the introduction and culture of this valuable fruit, we must say that there is in it a feature of decay called "blight," that appears all unknown. The most intelligent of horticulturist apparently have no explicit idea of what the blight is, or how it may be checked. Various remedies for the blight have been recommended, but no one proves a specific. A healthy growth of the tree, in a soil moist yet dry, i. e., void of stagnant water at the base of the roots, is about the only preventive.

As, with the apple, the selection of varieties has been made to meet the wants of the public rather than ministering to the fancy of amateurs. So, also, has our list been classed as to latitude, fully designated as to boundaries under head of the apple.

In the list of size, color, form, etc., we here also copy from the American Pomological Society's Catalogue, as follows :

The columns explain. *Size*—s. small ; l. large ; m. medium, *Flower*—p. pyriform ; r. o. p. roundish, obtuse pyriform ; r. a. p. roundish, acute pyriform ; ob. p. obtuse pyriform ; r. roundish ; r. ob. roundish obtuse. *Color*—y. g. yellow or yellowish green, with a red or russet-red cheek ; y. r. yellow and russet ; y. when mostly yellow or yellowish. *Quality*—g. good ; v. g. very good; b. best. *Use*—f. valuable family desert ; k. m. kitchen and market ; f. m. family and market. *Season*—s. summer ; l. s. late summer ; a. autumn ; e. a. early autumn ; l. a. late autumn; w. winter. *Origin*—En. English ; Am. American ; F. French ; Fl. Flemish ; B. Belgium ; H. Holland.

With apples, our list ranges ten to forty ; with pears we reduce and make it ten to thirty. Our list of the best is as follows :

CATALOGUE TABLE OF PEARS.

NAMES.	Size.	Form.	Color.	Quality.	Use.	Season.	Origin.	REMARKS.
Abbot,	m	ob p	y r	v g	f	e a	Am	One of value for the table
Ananas d'Ete,	l	p	y g	v g	f m	e a	H	As profitable as Bartlett.
Bartlett,	l	ob o p	y	v g	f m	l s	En	Well known
Belle Lucrative,	m	r o p	y g	v g	f m	e a	H	Very productive.
Beurre Bosc,	l	p	y g	b	f m	l a	B	One of the best.
Beurre Clairgeau,	l	p	y r	g	m	l a	F	Large and showy.
Beurre d'Anjou,	l	ob p	y g	v g	f m	l a	F	One of the best.
Beurre Giffard,	m	p	y g	v g	f m	s a	F	Profitable and good.
Beurre Superfin,	m	r p	y r	v g	f	a a	F	Valuable for family use.
Beurre Easter,	l	r ob p	y r	v g	f	w	B	Valuable in all south-west.
Beurre Diel,	l	r ob p	y r	v g	f m	l a	B	Good bearer and profitable.
Beurre Coit,	m	ob p	y r	b	f m	a	Am	Hardy and productive.
Bloodgood,	m	r	y r	v g	f	a	Am	A fine early variety.
Brandywine,	m	r o p	y g	v g	f m	s	Am	Esteemed where known.
Buffum,	m	r o p	y g r	g	m	e a	Am	A hardy tree.
Beurre Langlier,	m	ob p	y r	v g	f m	w	F	A fine winter sort.
Clapp's Favorite,	l	ob o p	y g	v g	f m	s	An	Now but of promise.
Dearborn's Seedling,	s	r p	y	v g	f	s	Am	Valuable for house use.
Doctor Reeder,	s	r o p	y r	b	f	l a	Am	One of best in quality.
Doyenne Boussock,	l	r o p	y r	v g	f m	e a	B	Profitable.
Doyenne de Comice,	l	r o p	y g	b	f m	l a	F	Esteemed where known.
Doyenne d'Ete,	s	r o p	y g	v g	f	s	B	One of the earliest pears.
Dana's Hovey,	s	r ob p	y g	b	f	w	Am	Fine for the family.
Duchess d'Angouleme	l	ob o p	y	v g	f m	a	F	One of the most profitable.
Emile de Heyst,	l	ob p	y r	b	f	l a	B	One of the best.
Fulton,	s	r ob	y r	v g	f	a	Am	Very hardy.

REMARKS.	Size.	Form.	Color.	Quality.	Use.	Season.	Origin.	REMARKS.
Flemish Beauty,	1	r ob p	y g	v g	f m	a	B	Profitable west.
Goodale,	1	r ob	y r	v g	f m	w	Am	A native of Maine.
Glout Morceau,	m	ob p	y	g	f	w		Valued south-west.
Howell,	1	r p	y g	v g	f m	e a	Am	Valued where known.
Josephine de Malines,	m	r ob p	y r	v g	f	w	F	A choice winter pear.
Jaminette,	m	r ob	y r	v g	f m	w		Old variety, hardy and good
Kirtland,	m	r ob	y r	v g	f m	e a	Am	Equal to Seckel.
Lawrence,	m	r o p	y r	v g	f m	w	Am	Profitable and hardy.
Louise Bon de Jersey,	m	ob p	y g	v g	f m	e a	F	One of the most profitable
Marechal de la Cour,	1	ob p	y g	v g	f m	a	F	Valuable.
McLaughlin,	1	ob p	y g	v g	f m	w	Am	One of the hardy sorts.
Mount Vernon,	m	p	y r	v g	f m	l a	Am	Of peculiar flavor.
Madeline,	m		y g	v g	f m		F	An old variety, valued.
Onondaga,	1	ob p	y g	v g	f m	l a	Am	Profitable.
Princes St. Germain,	m	r o p	y g	v g	f m	w	Am	One of the best varieties.
Rostiezer,	s	p	y g	b	f	s		Especially valuable
Seckel,	s	r	y g	b	f m	a	Am	Well known.
Sheldon,	m	r	y g	v g	f m	a	Am	One of the best.
Stevens' Gennessee,	1		y	v g	f m	e a	Am	Reliable.
St. Michael Archangel	1	r p	y g	g	f m	a	F	Saleable.
Saint Ghislain,	m	p	y	g	f	e a	B	Hardy and productive.
Tyson,	m	r o p	y g	g b	f m	s	Am	Valuable.
Vicar of Winkfield,	1	p	y	b	f	w	F	Profitable.
Winter Nelis,	m	ob p	y r	b	f m	w	B	Hardy and profitable.
White Doyenne,	m	ob p	y g	b	f m	a	F	Valued west.

Valuable north of 43 degrees of latitude for our range.
For the period of ripening, etc., see table :

Abbot, Ananas d'Ete, Bartlett, Belle Lucrative, Beurre
Bosc, Beurre d'Anjou, Beurre Diel, Beurre Giffard, Beurre
Superfin, Bloodgood, Brandywine, Buffum, Clapp's Favorite, Fulton, Dearborn's Seedling, Flemish Beauty, Doctor
Reeder, Howell, Kirtland, Lawrence, Louise Bonne de
Jersey, Onondaga, Tyson, Seckel, Winter Nelis, McLaughlin, Beurre Coit, Souvenier de Congress, Goodale,
Doyenne Boussock.

DOCTOR REEDER PEAR.

This exceedingly valuable new pear originated with Dr.
HENRY REEDER, Varick, Seneca county, N. Y., from
seed of a Winter Nelis pear, the tree of which grew near

a Seckel. The fruit in form resembles the Seckel, while, with the rich, honied sweetness of that variety, it has also the juicy, sprightly vivacity of the Winter Nelis. The original tree is about twelve years old, and as yet has been but little disseminated. We are indebted to Messrs. ELL-WANGER & BARRY of Rochester, N. Y., for specimens from which we have made the accompanying drawing and description. The variety is generally known under the name of Dr. Reeder's Seedling, by which it was noticed first in American Pomological Society's Transactions by CHARLES DOWNING.

Fruit small in size, globular, obtuse pyriform, pale yellow, mostly overspread with a smooth, warm, cinnamon russet,—stem slender, nearly three-fourths of an inch long, set in a broad, open, moderately deep cavity, having occasionally a slight lip on one side; calyx open, large for size of fruit, with erect, divided, rounded segments; basin shallow, broad, smooth and open; flesh yellowish white, fine grained, juicy, melting, almost buttery, sprightly, sweet, and slightly aromatic; *best* in quality; core medium; seeds blackish; season early November.

The list for latitude 43 down to 40, we advise the following:

Bartlett, Belle Lucrative, Beurre Bosc, Beurre Clairgeau, Beurre d'Anjou, Doyenne de Comice, Beurre Giffard, Beurre Superfine, Brandywine, Marechal de la Cour, Clapp's Favorite, Doyenne Boussock, Doyenne d'Ete, Duchess d'Angouleme, Flemish Beauty, Glout Morceau, Howell, Josephine de Malines, Kirtland, Louise bon de Jersey, Lawrence, Onondaga, Rostiezer, White Doyenne,

Seckel, Sheldon, Tyson, Stevens' Genesee, Vicar of Wakefield, Winter Nelis.

From latitude 40 down to 37, we offer the following as the best list:

Ananas d'Ete, Bartlett, Belle Lucrative, Beurre Bosc, Beurre Clairgeau, Beurre d'Anjou, Beurre Giffard, Beurre Langlier, Beurre Superfine, Clapp's Favorite, Dana's Hovey, Dearborn's Seedling, Doyenne de Comice, Marechal de la Cour, Emile de Heyst, Beurre Easter, Glout Morceau, Duchess d'Angouleme, Doctor Reeder, Josephine de Malines, Lawrence, Louise Bonne de Jersey, Mount Vernon, Onondaga, Rostiezer, Princes St. Germain, Tyson, and Winter Nelis.

From latitude 37 and below the following have repute: Bartlett, Belle Lucrative, Beurre Clairgeau, Beurre d' Anjou, Beurre Superfine, Bloodgood, Buffum, Brandywine, Doyenne d'Ete, Beurre Easter, Duchess d'Angouleme, Howell, Lawrence, Onondaga, Kirtland, Seckel, Doctor Reeder, Beurre Bosc, Beurre Giffard, Flemish Beauty, Rostiezer, St. Michael Archangel, Tyson, Winter Nelis, Madelaine, Dearborn's Seedling, Jaminette, Josephine de Molines, St. Ghislain.

PEARS

Warmer districts of the southern half of the country are more favourable for Pear-growing than the colder northern counties.

Early blossoms need protection in spring : maturing fruits require full sun.

In cold, exposed gardens the protection and warmth afforded by a wall or fence are essential for the production of well-ripened, good-quality fruit of most late-maturing varieties.

1. FORMS OF TRAINING, see p. 24

Standard trees are slow to arrive at good bearing : they are difficult to keep free from Scab (see p. 213) and unsuitable except for very hardy Pears, such as Chalk, Hessle, Beurré Clairgeau, etc.

Pyramid, bush trees and cordons are best for the open garden and plantation.

Espalier and cordon trees against a warm wall will bring the most delicate varieties to perfect maturity.

2. ROOT-STOCKS

The two main groups of stocks in common use are :
The seedling or Free Pear stocks for vigorous trees.
The Quince stocks for bush, pyramid and trained trees.

VIGOROUS STOCKS

Seedling or Free stocks, obtained mainly from Perry pomace, are extremely variable.

Selected seedlings are being classified and tested at East Malling and results may provide stocks suitable for all forms of trees.

At least four distinct varieties of Quince are in general use. Those recommended are :

Malling A (Angers Quince) — moderately vigorous : suitable for general purposes, pyramid, bush, espalier and cordon.

Malling B (Common Quince) — slightly more dwarfing.

Malling C — makes smallest and most precocious tree : excellent for cordons.

All are readily propagated vegetatively by layering.

Experiments at East Malling show there are varietal preferences for different strains or types of Quince stocks. Complete evidence is lacking, but, as has long been known, certain varieties do not unite and form a strong union with Quince and must be double-worked (see p. 130).

Varieties rarely making satisfactory union with Quince are : Jargonelle, Joséphine de Malines, Marguerite Marillat, Marie Louise, Souvenir de Congrès.

Varieties that make good union but are better double-worked are : Dr. Jules Guyot, Thompson's, William's Bon Chrétien.

Varieties making good union and used as ' intermediate ' stock for double-working are : Beurré d'Amanlis, Pitmaston Duchess, Uvedale's St. Germain.

Trees on Quince stock are prone to the evils of scion-rooting (see p. 36). At planting the tree must be set with union of stock and scion well above soil-level.

3. VARIETIES

A. FOR THE GARDEN AND PRIVATE GROWER

Comparatively few of the large number of varieties in cultivation are entirely satisfactory for garden planting.

In cold gardens the late autumn and winter varieties mature fruit of good quality only when grown against a sheltering wall or fence.

Doyenné du Comice is recognised as the most delicious of all Pears, though others, as Beurré Superfin, Thompson's, Seckle, rank very high in the estimation of the epicure.

Not all varieties of high quality are suitable for general planting and there are some first-quality Pears omitted from the following tables, which enumerate only those varieties most generally satisfactory.

(1) *Dessert varieties : for half-standards, pyramids and bushes :*

(arranged according to season for use)

Laxton's Superb	Émile d'Heyst
William's Bon Chrétien	Conference
Souvenir de Congrès	Doyenné du Comice
Beurré Superfin	Durondeau
Louise Bonne of Jersey	Beurré Diel
Beurré Hardy	Joséphine de Malines

(2) *Varieties of first-rate flavour and quality : for dwarf bushes, pyramids, cordons and espaliers :*

William's Bon Chrétien	Doyenné du Comice [1]
Beurré Superfin	Beurré Six [1]
Comte de Lamy	Winter Nélis [1]
Marie Louise	Duchess de Bordeaux [1]
Seckle	Bergamotte d'Espéren [1]
Thompson's [1]	Olivier de Serres [1]

(3) *Culinary varieties :*

(most dessert varieties have good culinary quality if gathered a little before fully ripe)

Beurré Capiaumont	Vicar of Winkfield
Pitmaston Duchess	Bellissime d'Hiver
Beurré Clairgeau	Catillac

B. FOR MARKET GROWERS

Few varieties combine satisfactory hardiness and fertility with high market value.

Doyenné du Comice is the market Pear of highest quality and commands highest prices, but it is not always the most profitable, because its crops are invariably smaller than those from hardier and more fertile varieties. Conference is generally regarded as the most satisfactory of all Pears for market : William's Bon Chrétien is a general favourite, and two other popular and profitable varieties are Pitmaston Duchess — the

[1] Specially deserving of wall space.

'monster' Pear — and Fertility, with little more than its enormous cropping powers to recommend it.

(1) *Recommended : for pyramids, bushes and cordons :*

Dr. Jules Guyot	Fertility
Laxton's Superb	Conference
William's Bon Chrétien	Pitmaston Duchess
Doyenné du Comice	Beurré Hardy

(2) *Varieties included in the National Mark Scheme of Marketing :*

(arranged alphabetically)

Beurré d'Amanlis	Fertility
Beurré Clairgeau	Glou Morceau
Beurré Hardy	Hessle
Catillac	Joséphine de Malines
Clapp's Favourite	Louise Bonne of Jersey
Conference	Marguerite Marillat
Dr. Jules Guyot	Marie Louise d'Uccle
Doyenné du Comice	Pitmaston Duchess
Émile d'Heyst	William's Bon Chrétien

Additional varieties grown for market are :

Beurré Diel	Beurré Superfin
Beurré Bosc	Souvenir de Congrès

(3) *Cheap Pears — as standards for planting as wind-break :*

Beurré Capiaumont	Jargonelle
Chalk	Hessle

4. CROSS-POLLINATION, see p. 90

see p. 90

The planting of large blocks of a single variety is to be avoided.

As with Apples and Plums, many varieties are self-sterile, others are only partially self-fertile. Even those varieties that rank as self-fertile will set heavier crops and will develop finer fruits when cross-pollinated than when dependent upon their own pollen.

Self - fertile Varieties. — Bellissime d'Hiver, Bergamotte d'Espéren, Beurré Bachelier, Conference, Dr. Jules Guyot,

Doyenné Bussoch, Durondeau, Hessle, Marie Louise, Marie Louise d'Uccle, Uvedale's St. Germain, William's Bon Chrétien.
Partially Self-fertile Varieties, but dependent upon cross-pollination for good cropping.—Comte de Lamy, Laxton's Superb, Louise Bonne of Jersey, Pitmaston Duchess, Marguerite Marillat.
Self-sterile Varieties.—Beurré Clairgeau, Beurré d'Amanlis, Catillac, Clapp's Favourite, Doyenné du Comice, Émile d'Heyst, Fertility, Glou Morceau, Joséphine de Malines, Olivier de Serres, Souvenir de Congrès, Thompson's, Vicar of Winkfield, Winter Nélis.

Cross-incompatibility does not exist among varieties of Pears, but the following varieties produce little good pollen and are therefore unsatisfactory pollinators : Beurré d'Amanlis, Beurré Diel, Catillac, Conseiller de la Cour, Marguerite Marillat, Pitmaston Duchess, Vicar of Winkfield, Uvedale's St. Germain.

For maximum fruit-setting, varieties which most nearly coincide in blossoming should be planted together.

Full flowering of the earliest and latest varieties is separated by about eighteen days.

Early flowering varieties, as a rule, remain in flower almost a week longer than do late flowering varieties : the average period over which a variety remains in flower is eighteen days.

In the following list and chart, varieties are grouped in order of flowering.

Horizontal lines in the chart represent the effective flowering period (here shortened to ten days) of varieties in each group.

The greater the overlap of the horizontal lines the more nearly the varieties in the corresponding groups coincide in flowering. For example, a variety in Group A would not be chosen as a pollinator for a variety in Group G, H or I, since lines corresponding to these groups do not overlap at all. Nor would a variety in Group B be chosen as a pollinator for one in Group H, and so on.

5. PEARS — ORDER OF FLOWERING

Group A. Doyenné Bussoch, Doyenné d'Été, Jargonelle, Madame Treyve.

Group B. Beurré d'Amanlis, Beurré Six, Souvenir de Congrès, Louise Bonne of Jersey.
Group C. Bergamotte d'Espéren, Beurré Bosc, Beurré Clairgeau, Conference, Émile d'Heyst, Uvedale's St. Germain.
Group D. Beurré Diel, Beurré Superfin, Citron des Carmes, Comte de Lamy, Duchess de Bordeaux.
Group E. Bellissime d'Hiver, Beurré Hardy, Marguerite Marillat, Olivier de Serres.
Group F. Beurré Capiaumont, Joséphine de Malines, Thompson's, Winter Nélis, Marie Louise d'Uccle.
Group G. Clapp's Favourite, Catillac, Fertility, Laxton's Superb, Seckle, William's Bon Chrétien.
Group H. Triomphe de Vienne, Dr. Jules Guyot, Hessle, Pitmaston Duchess.
Group I. Doyenné du Comice, Glou Morceau, Marie Louise.

PEARS — PERIOD OF FLOWERING

Group	Days — 0 1 2 3 4 5 6 7 8 9 10 11 12 13 14 15 16 17 18 19 20 21 22 23 24 25 26 27 28
A	———————
B	———————
C	———————
D	———————
E	———————
F	———————
G	———————
H	———————
I	———————

Days — 0 1 2 3 4 5 6 7 8 9 10 11 12 13 14 15 16 17 18 19 20 21 22 23 24 25 26 27 28

6. THINNING

Clusters should be thinned to single fruits.

Thinning should commence early : malformed and diseased specimens are the first to be removed.

Finest dessert Pears are thinned to leave fruits 5 ins. apart along the branch.

Surplus fruits are best removed with scissors to avoid danger of dislodging whole clusters and breaking spurs.

PEARS

Large-fruited varieties, such as Marguerite Marillat, Beurré Superfin, are thinned more severely than small-fruited varieties as Seckle, Comte de Lamy, etc.

7. PRUNING, see p. 79

MODIFIED ROUTINE

Varieties that make natural spurs freely (as do most) : prune hard to maintain vigour and strengthen spurs.

Dwarf bushes, pyramids, cordons, espaliers : space out spurs five inches apart along the branches ; shorten very long spurs by half or more.

Erect growers, such as Beurré Clairgeau, Dr. Jules Guyot, Marguerite Marillat, Seckle : prune leaders to outward-pointing bud ; thin branches to prevent overcrowding in centre of tree.

Tip-fruiting varieties — Jargonelle, Joséphine de Malines : prune lightly ; cut back only the crowded, awkwardly placed and unhealthy growths.

Dwarf and trained trees should be summer pruned (see p. 83) each season.

8. NOTES ON VARIETIES

The following list (pp. 208-211) details some of the more important characters of varieties commonly grown (see note under Apple, p. 164).

9. PESTS AND DISEASES

INSECT PESTS

(a) *Pear Midge* (*Contarinia pyrivora*).

The most serious pest of Pears : widespread.

Interior of fruitlets eaten out by small, whitish maggots.

Attacked fruitlets swell rapidly, become misshapen and usually show pronounced bulge on one side : skin cracked, blotched with black patches.

Fruits fall to ground : occasionally rot on tree.

When cut open, affected fruit shows blackened mass of dried pulp, with whitish grubs inside.

DESCRIPTIVE LIST OF VARIETIES

Variety	Fruit Size and Quality	Approximate Week for Picking	Season of Use	Vigour and Habit	Cropping	Other Characteristics
Bellissime d'Hiver	Large : culinary, first-rate	Oct. (2)	Dec.-Mar.	Vigorous : upright	Free : regular	Perhaps the best of all culinary varieties for garden : makes good standard
Bergamotte d'Espéren	Medium : rich flavour : perfumed	Oct. (2)	Feb.-Mar.	Vigorous : upright-spreading	Moderate	Best trained against warm wall
Beurré d'Amanlis	Medium to large : juicy : pleasantly flavoured	Aug. (4)	Early Sept.	Vigorous : spreading	Good	Hardy variety, succeeds where others fail. Used as 'intermediate' when double-working
Beurré Bosc	Large : juicy : fair quality	Sept. (1)	Sept.-Oct.	Moderate to weak : spreading	Good : regular	The Calebasse Pear of the markets (correct name Calabasse Bosc) : rather subject to Scab
Beurré Capiaumont	Rather small : poor dessert : good culinary	Sept. (1)	Sept.-Oct.	Moderately vigorous : little spreading	Free : reliable	Very hardy Pear : often grown as standard or half-standard for wind-break
Beurré Clairgeau	Large : culinary	Sept. (4)	Nov.-Dec.	Vigorous : upright-spreading	Heavy	Hardy : second-class culinary Pear for market. Subject to Scab
Beurré Diel	Large : excellent when well ripened	Sept. (1)	Oct.-Dec.	Vigorous : upright-spreading	Heavy : regular	Hardy; but requires warm season to perfect fruit : in cold, wet year quality is lacking
Beurré Hardy	Large : good flavour	Sept. (2)	Oct.	Vigorous : upright-spreading	Free : regular	Does well in all forms of training. Good market variety
Beurré Six	Large : juicy : sweet : first-class	Oct. (1)	Nov.-Dec.	Vigorous : upright-spreading	Regular : good	Excellent garden variety in any form of training. Shows resistance to Scab
Beurré Superfin	Medium : rich : sweet : perfumed flavour	Sept. (2)	Oct.	Moderately vigorous : little spreading	Good	One of the very best varieties. Gather before fully mature : apt to rot at core in store

Name	Size / Quality	Ripe	Season	Habit	Crop	Remarks
Catillac ·	Large : culinary	Oct. (9)		spreading stout branches	regular	until proper season. makes strong standard tree
Citron des Carmes	Small : sweet : lacking quality	July (4)	End July	Moderate to weak	Heavy	Best on vigorous stock. Poor quality ; useful for its earliness
Clapp's Favourite	Medium : fair quality ; juicy : sweet	Aug. (3)	End Aug.-early Sept.	Moderately vigorous : upright	Very good : regular	Free cropping market Pear of second quality
Comte de Lamy ·	Small : first-class flavour and quality	Sept. (2-3)	Oct.-early Nov.	Moderately vigorous : spreading	Good	Hardy reliable Pear of excellent quality for garden
Conference ·	Medium : (sometimes large)	Sept. (4)	Oct.-Nov.	Moderately vigorous : upright-spreading	Heavy : regular	Very popular for garden and market ; very fertile. Resists Scab. Best all-round Pear for garden and plantation
Dr. Jules Guyot ·	Medium : juicy : slight musk flavour	Aug. (3)	Early Sept.	Moderately vigorous : upright, compact	Heavy : regular	A good market variety ; resembles William's Bon Chrétien. Gather before quite ripe
Doyenné du Comice	Large : most deliciously flavoured : unequalled	Oct. (1)	Nov.	Moderately vigorous : upright-spreading	Irregular	The Cox's Orange Pippin of Pears. Requires warm, well-drained loam ; best as espalier or cordon against wall. Rather subject to Scab
Doyenné Ed'té ·	Small : very juicy : sweet	July (3)	July-early Aug.	Moderate to weak : upright-spreading	Very good	Valuable for its earliness
Duchess de Bordeaux	Medium : richly flavoured	Oct. (2)	Jan.-Mar.	Moderately vigorous : upright	Good	One of the best late Pears : requires wall to perfect fruits in cool garden
Durondeau ·	Large : good flavour when well grown	Sept. (4)	Oct.-Nov.	Moderately vigorous : upright, compact	Very good : regular	Does well in all forms of training. Most reliable. Autumn foliage dark reddish brown

Variety	Fruit Size and Quality	Approximate Week for Picking	Season of Use	Vigour and Habit	Cropping	Other Characteristics
Émile d'Heyst	Medium : good flavour : perfumed	Sept. (4)	Oct.-Nov.	Moderately vigorous to rather weak : spreading	Good : somewhat irregular	Hardy ; succeeds in all forms of training. Autumn foliage claret red. Subject to Pear Leaf Blister Mite
Fertility	Small : juicy : sweet : lacking quality	Sept. (2-3)	Oct.	Moderately vigorous : upright-spreading	Very heavy : regular	Grown in large quantities for market. Very subject to Scab and Canker. Autumn foliage crimson
Glou Morceau	Medium-large : rich flavour	Oct. (2)	Dec.-Feb.	Moderately vigorous : spreading	Good	Best trained against warm wall. Fruits ripen successionally in store : good keeper
Hessle	Small : juicy : sweet : lacking quality	Sept. (3)	Oct.	Moderately vigorous : upright-spreading	Heavy	A 'cheap' market Pear : good as standard ; succeeds where tender varieties fail
Jargonelle	Medium : juicy : sweet	Aug. (1)	Aug.	Fairly vigorous : spreading, straggling	Heavy : regular	Best as half-standard or pyramid. Gather before fully ripe ; soon decays. A 'tip fruiter'. Very subject to Scab
Joséphine de Malines	Medium to small : very good quality : perfumed	Oct. (1)	Dec.-Jan.	Vigorous : spreading, straggling	Heavy : regular	Best as half-standard — 'tip fruiter' ; most regular cropping late Pear and good keeper
Laxton's Superb	Medium : sweet : juicy : good quality	Aug. (4)	Early Sept.	Moderately vigorous : upright-spreading	Good	A new and valuable addition to the early Pears
Louise Bonne of Jersey	Medium : very good flavour and quality	Sept. (3)	Oct.	Moderately vigorous : upright-spreading	Good : regular	Succeeds in any form of training : popular market variety
Marguerite Marillat	Very large : juicy : pleasantly flavoured	Sept. (1)	Sept.	Vigorous : upright : very stout	Very heavy : regular	Popular market variety : requires hard spur-pruning. Autumn foliage bright red

Name	Description / Flavour		Season	Habit	Cropping	Remarks
	quality: distinct flavour			vigorous: spreading	uncertain: sometimes very good	Doyenne du Comice
Marie Louise d'Uccle	Fairly large: delicate flavour	Sept. (2)	Oct.	Moderately vigorous: compact: little spreading	Good: regular	Rather subject to Scab
Olivier de Serres	Medium: brisk, musky flavour	Oct. (2)	Feb.-Mar.	Moderately vigorous to dwarf	Irregular	Requires warm wall to mature fruit to perfection
Pitmaston Duchess	Very large: pleasantly flavoured: good stewing Pear	Sept. (4)	Oct.-Nov.	Vigorous: upright-spreading	Regular: good	A popular variety for dessert and culinary use: very subject to Scab. Autumn foliage turns dark red
Seckle	Small: very sweet: rich flavour: first-class	Sept. (4)	Oct.-Nov.	Rather weak: upright	Fairly reliable	Excellent Pear; best on vigorous stock
Souvenir de Congrès	Large: sweet: musky flavour	Sept. (1)	Sept.	Moderately vigorous: compact	Good: little irregular	Best on Pear stock or double-grafted
Thompson's	Medium to large: first-rate	Sept. (3)	Oct.-Nov.	Moderately vigorous: upright-spreading	Irregular	A most delicious Pear: best against warm wall
Triomphe de Vienne	Medium to large: very juicy: good	Sept. (1)	Sept.	Fairly vigorous: little spreading	Very good	A useful early variety: best on vigorous stock. Autumn foliage brilliant red
Vicar of Winkfield	Very large: culinary	Oct. (2)	Dec.-Jan.	Very vigorous: semi-upright	Good: regular	A stewing Pear, rarely fit for dessert. Makes good standard
William's Bon Chrétien	Medium to rather large: very juicy: sweet: strong musky flavour	Aug. (4)	Sept.	Moderately vigorous: little spreading	Good: regular	Very popular for garden and market. Gather before fully ripe, finish in cool store. Autumn foliage crimson
Winter Nélis	Medium: richly flavoured	Oct. (1)	Nov.-Jan.	Little weak: spreading	Regular	Best on vigorous stock: requires wall to bring fruit to perfection

The midges deposit eggs in flowers : newly hatched maggots eat into young, immature fruits.

Control.—Pick off and burn all malformed, abnormally swollen fruitlets.

Spray with Nicotine soap when flowers are in full bloom to kill eggs.

Run pigs beneath trees during early spring and summer months or cultivate the ground thoroughly from mid-June to late July to expose and kill maggots.

[Early-flowering varieties usually suffer more severely than late-flowering varieties, but Doyenné du Comice is rarely badly attacked.]

(b) Pear Leaf Blister Mite (Eriophyes piri).

Widespread : becoming more prevalent.

Upper surface of young leaves covered with small, yellow-green and reddish blisters. Leaves turn brown or black and die during summer.

Young fruits may be attacked, causing malformation and early dropping.

The minute mites burrow into young leaves, raising blisters in which eggs deposited. Mites winter beneath bud scales.

Control.—Spray with Lime-sulphur (1–20) in early March.

(c) Pear Slugworm (Caliroa limacina).

Slimy, shining, slug-like maggots feed on upper surface of leaves.

Foliage becomes blotched and partly skeletonized.

Adult insect is a Sawfly : appears early in summer and deposits eggs in slits made in leaf surface.

(Also attacks Cherries.)

Control.—Spray with Lead arsenate in summer : or, if within a month of fruit ripening, spray with non-poisonous insecticide, Derris, etc.

(d) Winter Moths (see p. 175).

(e) Aphis (see p. 172).

(f) Apple Blossom Weevil (see p. 174).

(g) Red Spider (see p. 173).

(h) Tortrix Moth (see p. 175).

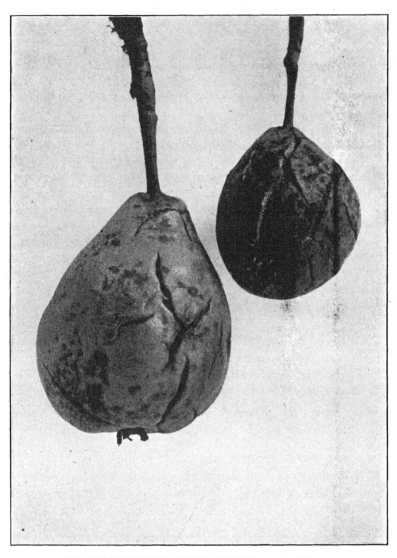

PEARS INFECTED WITH SCAB (*Venturia pirina*)

FUNGOID DISEASES

(a) *Pear Scab* (*Venturia pirina*).

Widespread : most serious disease of Pears.

Closely allied to Apple Scab (see p. 176).

Fruits patched with black spots and scabs : split and deeply cracked.

Control.—Spray with Bordeaux Mixture or Lime-sulphur (1–30) immediately before flowers open.

Spray second time as soon as flowering is over, with Bordeaux Mixture or Lime-sulphur (1-80), and if necessary a third time a fortnight later.

If infection bad, dusting with Copper-lime may be necessary during summer months.

Prune and burn diseased shoots and spurs showing blistered bark, in winter.

Varieties *most susceptible* are : Beurré Clairgeau, Beurré d'Amanlis, Doyenné du Comice, Fertility, Glou Morceau, Pitmaston Duchess, Souvenir de Congrès, William's Bon Chrétien.

Variety showing *greatest resistance* : Conference.

(b) *Canker* (see under Apple, see p. 178).

Pears only occasionally attacked : often follows Scab.

Most susceptible varieties : Fertility and Marie Louise.

(c) *Brown Rot, Blossom Wilt, Wither Tip* (see under Apple, p. 178).

SEASONAL CONTROL MEASURES

The most important measure is spraying in spring to control Scab : other measures are necessary only when pests are troublesome.

Winter

January : Cut off all diseased and dead wood. Search carefully and remove all shoots infected with Scab.

Spray with Tar-oil wash (5 to 7 per cent) in winter to clean bark and destroy aphis eggs (seldom necessary every winter).

March : Spray with Lime-sulphur (1–20) against Pear Leaf Blister Mite.

April–May : Spray with Bordeaux Mixture or Lime-sulphur at white-bud stage to prevent Scab.

Spray with Bordeaux Mixture or Lime-sulphur at petal-fall stage against Scab. Add Nicotine if aphis present.

Summer

June : Collect and burn malformed, swollen fruits attacked by Pear Midge. If this pest is prevalent in orchard, run pigs beneath trees.

Autumn

September : Grease-band stems if caterpillars of Winter Moth, etc., infest the trees.

PEARS

ALTHOUGH pears give me more pleasure to grow and
joy to eat than any other fruits, I shall only deal with
them briefly because their cultivation is identical in
many instances with that of apples.

SOIL AND ASPECT

A well-drained garden in which vegetables flourish will suit almost all varieties. They grow best in the south of Great Britain because they like warmth. A south wall is an excellent support for all kinds, trained as espaliers or cordons. Pitmaston Duchess and Durondeau particularly appreciate sunshine. Doyenne du Comice, Roosevelt, Conference, Beurre Bedford, Beurre Hardy, Easter Beurre, Beurre Superfin, and Marguerite Marillat succeed well against an east or a west, as well as against a south wall. Alternatively, all will grow well as small bush trees or pyramids in a sheltered garden. But the best quality pears invariably come from trees protected by walls.

VARIETIES

There are scores of excellent varieties. Of them all I prefer the above ten. Descriptions can be found in any good catalogue.

Doyenne du Comice is in the pear world what Cox's Orange Pippin is in apples, and is ready to eat in the same season. A dish each of these upon the table in November are the highest awards a fruit grower can wish for. But just like the premier apple, this pear is not one of the easiest to grow. Cross-fertilisation is necessary, and I would only plant it if I had Conference and Pitmaston Duchess also. The best variety by itself is Conference. In the order of preference I would put after Conference—Beurre Bedford, Pitmaston Duchess, Doyenne du Comice,

Beurre Superfin, Marguerite Marillat, Roosevelt, Beurre Hardy, Easter Beurre, and Durondeau. That order is not for quality as much as the way they would be added to a collection. If still more are wanted, further reliable varieties are—Emile d'Heyst, William's Bon Chrétien, Louise Bonne of Jersey, and Triomphe de Vienne. Although many of these varieties will ripen in the natural pear season, some will be ready earlier or later.

STOCKS

As with apples, plums, peaches, and cherries, pears must be grafted. Just as there are two types of root-stocks for apples, so with pears there are the Wild Pear and quince. The quince is the equivalent of the paradise in that it causes dwarfishness and is generally best in a small garden. It also causes fruits to be better coloured. A Pitmaston Duchess is green on " Wild Pear," but assumes lovely hazel markings on quince. The desirable russeting is more pronounced in some other varieties when the roots are quince stock. At least, I find it so ; therefore, unless large trees are wanted, the nurseryman is always asked for trees on quince stock.

Some growers double-graft certain varieties. That simply means that the young trees are regrafted after they begin to grow. There is no doubt that this operation is fascinating, but, in my opinion, it is merely sufficient to know of its existence when PLAIN FRUIT GROWING. The man who is anxious to practise such an art is strongly urged to learn how to grow trees and obtain fruits before he starts upon grafting. After he has proved himself a grower he can learn from larger books and by practical demonstration how to practise the art in many ways. He certainly should not worry about it when he begins growing pears. Trees of all shapes, *i.e.* bushes, cordons, pyramids, and espaliers, are generally well trained by nurserymen and are far superior to those he is likely to perpetrate himself.

PLANTING

The best time of year to plant is November, although it can be done at any time between leaf fall and spring. The procedure is exactly the same as for apples. Distances are also the same.

FEEDING

Pears like nitrogen, especially when the trees are apt to remain stunted through the overproduction of fruiting spurs. A light dressing of chicken manure once every two years in winter-time will supply that. An alternate supply can be ensured by dressing the soil over the roots with sulphate of ammonia in February instead.

Sulphate of potash or kainit or wood ashes will provide potash if applied in winter every two years, say.

Phosphates can be added in the form of bone meal mixed with the soil at planting time, or a little superphosphate of lime given as a dressing with the potash fertiliser.

Pruning for pears is very similar to that described for apples, but varieties are more individualistic and the pruner must use his discretion. Some trees will produce long thin shoots that will need drastic summer pruning to cause " spurring." Other trees will simply be a mass of fruiting spurs and will produce no " growing " wood. Both extremes are bad. A tree should be encouraged to grow a little each year and the end shoot of each espalier branch or the top of a cordon or the tips of bush or pyramid branches should extend farther afield each year.

We must be careful how we prune a strong tree, and not cut too much off or it will continue to produce many wood shoots each year instead of forming fruiting spurs. At the other extreme, the trees that produce clusters of fruiting spurs and no long wood shoots can often be induced to grow moderately by the removal of some of the overcrowded bunches of fruit spurs during wintertime.

Knowing which are wood shoots and which are fruiting spurs is the secret of correct action. Perhaps the best way to ascertain this is to study the trees in summer-time. Those short stubbly growths with three or more leaves growing together in a cluster are fruiting spurs, although they do not always bear fruit, while the shoots dotted with single leaves are wood or growing shoots. This also applies to apples.

Incidentally, another item that should have been dealt with under apples is the selection of pruning instruments.

A sharp, well-made secateur is better than a sharp knife. A sharp knife is better than a bad secateur. Both bad knives and bad secateurs are dangerous. There are a few excellent modern secateurs in popular use to-day that have made pruning a pleasure. One of these that I use most frequently is known as the Kelson Drawcut Pruner. I do not know who manufactures it. I bought it from a store and, although I have other makes in the tool cupboard, this one is brought out most often.

A small pruning saw is also necessary to cut off thick branches. It should be thin and have only one row of small teeth that will cut finely. Some saws have teeth along both edges. These are unnecessary and dangerous in clumsy hands.

A sharp knife is an essential part of the equipment as a sawn surface should always be pared off neatly afterwards to make it difficult for water, fungi, and insects to establish themselves within the wood tissues.

ROOT PRUNING

As quince stocks are naturally shallow-rooting, root pruning is seldom necessary. On the other hand, the Wild Pear stock has a bad habit of sending long roots into the deep soil and that is often the cause of unfruitfulness. If a tree grows strongly and bears plenty of blossoms, and cross-fertilisation is not faulty, the trouble can generally be traced to tap-roots. The remedy is to root-prune by the method described for apples. Remember the quarter-circle for wall trees.

FRUIT THINNING

Pears, like apples, are inclined to bear heavy crops of small fruits some years, and none in others unless thinning is done. As we know well, the fruiting spurs bear a cluster of leaves and, in addition, usually a rosette of blossoms. Many of these blossoms fail to " set fruit," and ultimately fall off. Those that remain eventually form into tiny fruits, some of which drop off without any fuss. That is Nature's way of thinning. Then we remove more still, so that only one is left upon a spur to grow into a large good specimen. This treatment also induces the trees to bear regularly and steadily instead of erratically. The hints upon thinning apples give the rest of the information necessary. Never shirk doing this job.

FROST PROTECTION

Very often a crop of apples or pears, or plums, or peaches is doomed when blossoms are frozen. Market growers try to combat it in different ways. We can do so easily because our trees are small in size and numbers. The tennis-court net, or hessian, or any light material rigged over the trees in the blossom period, will be all that is necessary to keep light spring frosts away.

Just like apples, too, early pears need gathering before they part readily from the tree and ripening in a cool room. One of the bothers of ripening pears is that they go " sleepy " before the outer skin denotes ripeness. This is less likely if the early varieties are kept cool while they are ripening. One soon begins to know by feeling the end near the stalk and by appearances when a pear has reached the day of perfection. Some varieties are not so troublesome as others. Doyenne du Comice, for instance, ripens slowly in the storeroom and is delightful for a longer period than the earlier Beurre Hardy which makes up its mind too hurriedly.

Latest pears, including Doyenne du Comice, should be kept upon the trees to the utmost limits and the system of putting perforated muslin bags over them and securing each to the tree with a slip-string adopted. This saves the trouble of collecting often and baulks birds. (See Apples.)

There is no practical way of colouring pears like there is for apples, but they can be made mellow more quickly by burying them in a box of hay, placing a board upon the hay inside the top of the box and placing a weight upon the board. Examine frequently.

I store my late pears in the fruit-room on a rack specially constructed. Lacking that convenience, I should probably adopt the method of a long-ago gardener who wrote :

" Get some unglazed jars—garden pots will do ;

make them perfectly clean if they have ever been used. Gather your pears very carefully. Put them on a dry sweet shelf to sweat. When that is over rub with a dry cloth as if you were dry-rubbing a baby. As soon as dry, put them one over the other into the jars without any sort of packing, close up the mouth of the jar loosely by placing a piece of slate over it, and stow away in a darkish frost-proof closet. Open the jars now and then to see how they are getting on. Do not put more than one sort in a jar if you can help it. Mind—the warmer they are kept, the faster they will ripen." (Note that this old gardener likened fruit growing to nursing, too !)

DISEASES AND PESTS

To go into details about pear pests would take up too much space. It is unnecessary to do so, but as is the case with the apples, it is essential to know that there are pear pests and that the spraying programme for apples is the best antidote to most of them. Grease-banding is also recommended, and, of course, Derris dust when any outward signs of mischief are noticed.

A peculiar pest of pears is known as the Pear Midge. Signs of it are a wholesale fall of fruit when about as large as hazel nuts. These, when cut open will reveal small pasty-coloured maggots. If no maggots, the cause is different, but if there are, all fallers should be picked up without delay and burned. The insect passes part of its life in the ground. Another safeguard is to skim a few inches of top soil away in uly and replace with fresh soil not infected. The Ministry of Agriculture recommends keeping poultry round the trees in spring when the insects are upating.

Pruning Pear Trees

AMATEURS will find little difficulty in pruning pear trees, for they are more uniform in growth than apple trees, and therefore require less discrimination in the use of the pruning knife. The grower who prunes his trees merely by the rule-of-thumb method, without exercising judgment, and without altering his system to suit the variety in question, will achieve greater success with pear than with apple trees; most of them are suited by the orthodox plan of summer and winter pruning already described in the chapter dealing with pruning apple trees.

Young pear trees usually grow very vigorously during the first few years after planting, and unless the precaution is taken to lift them annually in the autumn for the first three years and to shorten the thick roots they may before long become almost unmanageable, or, at least, such a thicket of growth that it will be difficult to bring them again into a fruit-bearing condition. The annual lifting and slight root-pruning ought to be considered essential, for it will be very difficult to regulate the growth of the young pear trees by branch-pruning only. If, however, their vigour is restricted in the way described while they are young they will gradually settle down, and once they begin to bear fruit crops with fair regularity this in itself assists in restricting the luxuriant growth of branches.

Pyramid Pear tree: prune at (*e*) in winter

Pear trees ought not to be planted in rich ground; no manure is required at planting time when the land is being prepared for them, but it may be put on the soil with advantage in early summer for the purpose of keeping the roots moist in hot weather.

In pruning standard pear trees the advice given in the chapter on pruning standard fruit trees should be followed, and for cordon pear trees the chapter dealing with this form of tree should be consulted.

The ordinary pear tree for planting in the open garden is usually in the form of a pyramid; that is to say, it has a main central stem on which branches develop almost from the base to the top. The pear tree is naturally of a pyramidal shape, and the form of tree known as a pyramid is the most suitable. The pear tree does not show nearly so much variation in manner of growth as the apple tree; some varieties of the latter make upright trees, others form rounded trees, while the branches of some are of drooping growth.

Orthodox Methods of Pruning

If the other details of cultivation referred to—annual lifting and root-pruning for the first few years and planting in suitable soil—are attended to, the orthodox method of summer and winter pruning will suit the pear tree. In July or early August the side shoots on the main branches are shortened to within about six leaves of the base of the current summer's growth, and in winter they are cut back farther to within two buds or so. That sounds very simple, and so indeed it is, but it is not quite enough.

PRUNING PEAR TREES

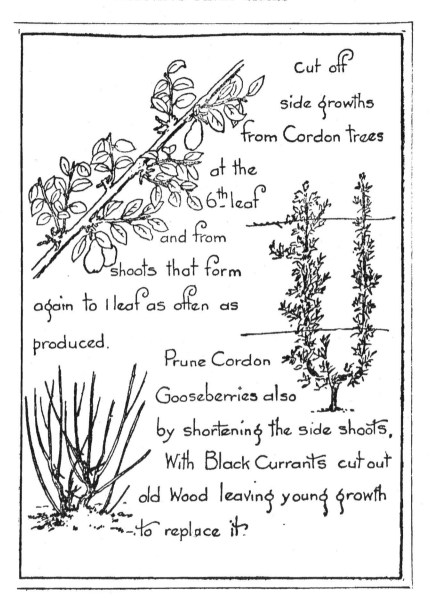

Cut off side growths from Cordon trees at the 6th leaf and from shoots that form again to 1 leaf as often as produced.

Prune Cordon Gooseberries also by shortening the side shoots. With Black Currants cut out old Wood leaving young growth to replace it.

The pear tree is a sun-lover, and unless the branches are kept well apart and the tree itself is in a sunny posi-tion, it may make a lot of growth, but fail to bear fruit freely. Above all things, see that all thin and weakly shoots inside the tree are cut right out in summer and winter so that the centre of the tree is open. Fresh

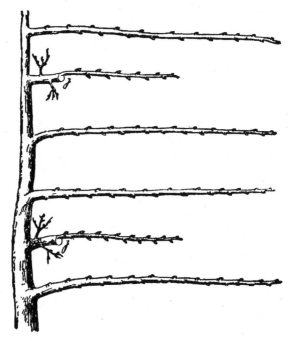

Old horizontal espalier of Pear; young shoots will grow if older, worn-out branches are cut as at (*j*)

shoots must not be allowed to grow at all unless it is intended that they shall develop into new branches for which there is room or unless they are to form fruit spurs and are pruned in summer and in winter; they should be cut right out before they have made much growth.

The aim of the pruner, not only in dealing with pear trees, but with all other fruit-trees, should be to obtain a tree with a limited number of main branches so wide apart that the fruit spurs on which blossom buds develop shall be open to the maximum of sunshine and air. Such treatment, combined with the usual process of summer and winter pruning, ought to produce satisfactory results, and is likely to do away with the necessity for severe cutting back, which is not to be recommended.

If the tree grows luxuriantly and bears little fruit it is not of much avail to continue cutting back the branches and shoots, for that will simply aggravate matters. The solution should rather be sought in thinning out, in root-pruning, and in correcting too rich a soil by the application of basic slag and superphosphate of lime instead of farmyard or stable manure.

PEARS FOR SMALL GARDENS

THE pear is not quite so reliable and serviceable as its rival, the apple. There are much fewer districts favourable for growing the choicest dessert pears than for apples. Some of the coarser varieties, suitable only for cooking, may be grown almost anywhere, but there is seldom room for them in the small garden.

The bush form of tree is quite suitable for pears. These should be planted from 15 feet to 18 feet apart. At present we have no stock for pears corresponding to the Jeune de Metz apple stock, quince being the best dwarfing stock available. With the exception of a few varieties, all bushes should be worked on quince. The exceptions referred to are varieties, named later, which bear such heavy crops that, unless they are on a rich soil, a vigorous stock is required to make them grow freely.

A few varieties do not grow well direct on quince, so the principle of double grafting is used. Another variety is grafted on to the quince stock. Then it is grafted with the variety required.

As the pear naturally spurs up freely, it is much more amenable to severe forms of training than is the apple. It makes excellent cordons, and does very well on a wall. All trained trees should be on quince stock.

Standards and half-standards, useful in poultry runs, etc., should be planted 20 feet to 24 feet apart. They may be on seedling pear stocks.

DESSERT VARIETIES.—*Doyenné d'Eté.*—Ripe at the end of July or early in August, and valuable on that account. A small pear of good flavour.

Clapp's Favourite.—A heavy cropper, ripening at the end of August or early in September. Unfortunately, it is rather liable to scab, but the fruit is of fair quality. It should be picked before it is quite ripe, or it goes mealy in the centre.

Laxton's Superb.—A large pear of good quality. It crops well, and is ripe early in September.

Marguerite Marillat.—A very large pear of fair quality, ripe in September. A good pear for the small garden, as it is a very heavy cropper.

Williams' Bon Chrétien.—Best known simply as "Williams." It ripens in September, and is the best-flavoured early variety. Probably Williams is the most widely known pear of all.

Souvenir de Congrès.—Ripe in September. The fruit is of good quality, large, with a musky flavour.

Fertility.—The quality of this variety is only moderate, but it carries enormous crops. It is ripe late in September or early in October. Except on very rich soil bushes should be on pear stock.

Louise Bonne of Jersey.—A heavy and regular cropper. The fruit, which is ripe in October, is of good quality, and has quite a distinctive and pleasing flavour.

Beurré Hardy.—Ripe at the end of October. It is very hardy and a good cropper. The fruit is of good quality. Apparently this variety is resistant to scab.

Conference.—Ripe at the end of October. A reliable, heavy-cropping pear, one of the most regular we have. It is advisable to grow bushes on pear stock. A good pollinator for self-sterile sorts.

Dorondeau.—A reliable pear, cropping regularly and heavily. Ripe in October or November.

Doyenne du Comice.—The finest-quality pear grown. Unfortunately, it is not a regular cropper. If possible, it should be grown on a wall.

Beurré Six.—A good pear for late use. It shows resistance to scab. The fruit is large, and of excellent quality.

It may not be out of place here to note that, with the exception of the earliest varieties, dessert pears should not be allowed to ripen on the tree. They should be picked a few days before they are ripe and kept until fit to use.

CULINARY VARIETIES.—Stewing pears can be grown in many districts where the dessert kinds do not succeed. In this country they do not ripen on the tree, but should be picked in October and stored until needed. For cooking it is not necessary for the fruit to be in the soft ripe stage.

Pitmaston Duchess.—The largest pear of all. It is a heavy cropper, and is often grown as a dessert variety, though the flavour is not always good.

Vicar of Winkfield.—A large pear, for use in December and January. A heavy cropper.

Catillac.—Said to keep until April. It is a large pear and a reliable cropper.

Bellisme d'Hiver.—May be used from November to March. It is one of the best cooking pears and is very prolific. The tree is vigorous, and makes natural spurs freely.

THE PEAR

Pears are Particular. Note that :

1. The Quince stock can make all the difference.
2. There is much to learn *re* " Scion rooting."
3. You can leave the fruit too long on the trees.
4. You shouldn't store apples and pears together.
5. Marie Louise doesn't want a mate !

PEARS can be grown on similar soil to apples, and perhaps the only difference is that far more attention has to be paid to climate. I suppose the ideal soil would be described as deep, warm, and moisture holding. Pears are easier to grow in districts where there is an equable temperature, and this means usually the southern half of England and Wales and areas alongside large bodies of water—two examples of this being the Medway Valley and Swale estuary, in Kent and the Acton Bridge area in Cheshire. Most pears prefer a warm, well-drained soil, which is not too dried-up in summer. The best late keeping pears such as Winter Nelis and Admiral Gervais need a sunny position and perfect shelter ; in addition of course, they like a dry ripening season. This is the reason that in mid and South France they grow pears better than we do. Therefore, unless a gardener can guarantee all these conditions it is better not to grow the best quality late keeping kinds but to concentrate on the more hardy types of what may be termed mid-season pears. I refer to Laxton's Superb, Conference, Williams, Dr. Jules Guyot and others which will be found on studying the lists given on pages 71–74. The variety Conference is not very particular as to soil.

In a small garden it should be possible to grow pears, providing the warmest situation can be chosen and protection given from cold winds. The pear blossoms much earlier than the apple and is therefore more likely to be damaged by frost. Pollination may be said to be a matter of minutes—shelter is therefore important so as to encourage bees and other insects that will do this work.

Stocks.—There are two main groups of stocks for pears—the wild pear, sometimes known as the free pear, and the quince. The wild-pear stock is used for standard trees and the quince stock for bush trees and pyramids. Espaliers and cordons should be grown on quince stocks also.

The East Malling Research Station has classified the quince stocks into five types :

Malling A, which is perhaps the commonest of the quince stocks used, produces good anchorage roots and much fibre. Much incompatibility between quince root stocks and pear varieties occurs, but Quince A is compatible with more varieties than any other.

Malling B, which is more dwarfing than A, and seems to be preferable for the general run of vigorous bush pears. It is particularly suited to Beurré Hardy.

Malling C, a dwarfing stock, which brings varieties into bearing early. It does not, however, seem to agree with all soils.

Malling D, which is not to be recommended, as it seems to give poor yields.

Malling E, a vigorous stock which is not much used.

The advantage of using a stock like Quince A or B means that a comparatively early cropping tree can be produced. It might be possible to liken the Malling C stock to the Type IX stock for apples and the Malling B quince to Type II stock for apples (see page 29), though differences are less marked with quince root stocks.

As mentioned before, it is unfortunately difficult to guarantee that all pear varieties will make a satisfactory union with a quince stock. The result is that it is necessary to purchase the following varieties " double worked." This means that a variety that *will* unite with the quince stock is grafted on first, and the incompatible variety is then grafted on top of the compatible variety.

THE PEAR

Dr. Jules Guyot.	Marguerite Marillat.
Jargonelle.	Souvenir de Congrès.
Joséphine de Malines.	Thompson's.
Marie Louise.	William's Bon Chrétien.

The following three varieties are usually used as intermediates :

Beurre d'Amanlis.	Pitmaston Duchess.
Uvedale's St Germain.	

Naturally, nurserymen charge more for double-worked trees.

Manuring.—It is difficult to know what to say about the manuring of pears, for little experimental work has been done on this subject. On the whole, though, it is possible to treat pears in the same way as apples. Pears, however, do not suffer from potash starvation as easily as apples and require higher nitrogenous conditions, usually provided by clean cultivation. On all soils the regular application of organic manure such as composted vegetable refuse is advisable, especially when growth shows a decline. The organic matter is put around the trees as a mulch in May and is cultivated into the ground in the early winter. Steamed Bone Flour and Bone Meal have given good results on heavy soils when used at 4–5 ounces to the square yard.

Grafting and Budding.—Pears are propagated by budding in the open in July and early August or by grafting in late March or early April on Wild Pear or Quince stocks.

Types of Trees.—As in the case of apples, pears may be planted as standards in grass orchards, as half standards in the garden and the poultry run or in the arable orchard, as bush trees when they will be trained in the same way as apples, and as cordons. They are one of the most popular fruits grown as espaliers, especially as they enjoy the warmth and protection of a wall. They are often grown also as pyramids on 2-ft. stems.

Pears require the full sun exposure if they are to be fully flavoured—that is why trained forms of trees are so often used. Pears are slow to come into bearing.

Age for Planting.—The best results are obtained from planting one- or two-year-olds or in the case of standards or half standards, three-year-olds.

Time of Planting.—As for apples. In the autumn preferably or if this is impossible, very early in the spring.

Planting.—The principle of planting may be carried out as advised in Chapter I, but the greatest care should be taken to see that the junction of stock and scion is well above the level of the soil. Pears scion root quickly, and the scion-rooted pear tree grows all to wood, throwing strong upright branches. It is useless to graft a pear on a dwarfing quince stock and then to allow the effect to be ruined by deep planting (see diagrams, page 65).

Pears on Pear Stock should be planted 25 feet apart in the case of the standards and 18 ft. apart in the case of bush trees. Bush and Pyramid trees on Quince A should be 18 ft. apart and bushes on C 12 ft. apart. Pears spur well and so are ideal as cordons planted 2 ft. apart.

Distance Apart.—Standards and half-standards on pear stocks should be planted from 18–25 feet apart each way, according to soils and varieties.

Bush trees and pyramids on quince stocks need to be at least 12 feet apart as a rule and 15 feet square would be even better.

Cordons will be planted 2 feet apart in the row, with the rows 6 feet apart.

Double cordons will need 5 feet in the rows.

Fuseau trees on Quince C stock can be planted as close as 6 feet by 6 feet.

Espalier trained trees should be 18 feet apart.

Pruning.—On the whole, the principles of pruning are the same as those outlined for apples, but, fortunately, most varieties of pear throw fruit spurs very readily.

Winter.—The leaders will be cut back by about half for the first four or five years, and the laterals or side growths by three-quarters. Once the trees get established it may only be necessary to tip the leaders by one-quarter, but it is usually necessary to do more in order to maintain vigour.

When the trees get old, the spurs tend to get rather long, and it may be necessary to (a) thin the spurs out (see diagram, page 40), or (b) cut back the long spur to a fruit bud lower down (see diagram, page 40).

Summer Pruning.—The same rules apply as for apples (see page 43).

Pruning the Young Tree.—As for apples (see page 36).

Subsequent Pruning.—Some branch thinning may be necessary, or a branch pulled out of shape may be sawn back to be replaced by a lateral, if one occurs in a suitable place and direction. Some varieties need fairly hard pruning to maintain vigour. Very tall branches may be lowered by cutting back to a fairly upright lateral.

Factors which Influence Pruning.—As for apples (see page 39).

Spurring _v._ Regulating.—It is seldom that pears are grown on the regulated system, and spur pruning may be carried out even on half-standard trees. It is possible, of course, to grow standard trees the " regulated " way, though the fruit obtained is by no means of such good quality.

Shaping and Forming.—As for apples (see page 36).

Habits of Trees.—Some varieties, like Conference, Dr. Jules Guyot, and Marguerite Marillat, tend to be too upright in their growth, and so care should be taken to cut always to an outward bud and to keep the centre of the tree open, though in very young trees leaving in the centre pushes the other branches outward, and the centre is then gradually opened. Other varieties, like William's Bon Chrêtien, tend to be too spreading, and so the leaders may have to be cut to an inward bud, though not when young.

Varieties which bear on the tips are Jargonelle and Josephine de Malines.

Root Pruning.—As for apple (see page 44).

Cordons and Espaliers.—As for apple. The leader or extension shoot should be tipped in the winter by removing one-third of its growth. This tipping ensures adequate fruit bud development. After the third year tipping may be omitted. The laterals should be treated as for apples, see page 44.

Pollination.—The pollination problem in the case of pears is very acute ; most of the varieties are self-sterile, and many of the others are only partially self-fertile. As most of the self-fertile varieties will crop far more heavily when they are cross-pollinated' it is proposed, for the purpose of this book, to classify them as self-sterile.

Fortunately with pears, almost any variety flowering at the same time as another may act as a pollinator, though there are certain varieties which produce little pollen, and so are not considered useful for this purpose.

The following are self-fertile varieties :—

Bellissime d'Hiver.	**Durondeau.**
Bergamotte d'Esperen.	**Hessle.**
Beurré Bachelier.	**Marie Louise.**
Conference.	**Marie Louise d'Uccle.**
Dr. Jules Guyot.	**Uvedale's St. Germain.**
Doyenne Bussoch.	**William's Bon Chrêtien.**

and the rest may be considered self-sterile.

The following varieties produce little pollen :

Beurré d'Amanlis.	**Marguerite Marillat.**
Beurré Diel.	**Pitmaston Duchess.**
Catillac.	**Vicar of Winkfield.**
Conseiller de la Cour.	**Uvedale's St. Germain.**

In order to determine which varieties are suitable pollinators for others, it is necessary to know approximately when they flower. For this reason the pears have been put into classes, and the period in which each class flowers is clearly defined by the chart, page 75.

Bark Ringing.—This is just as effective on pears as on apples. For details of the method, see Chapter XVIII.

Cultivation.—General cultivation—as for apples. But in addition note the following :—

Pears are so often grown against walls because of the warmth of protection that many varieties need, but they find these situations very dry. The gardener will, therefore, give his

Summer pruning.
Cutting back the laterals "hard."

Thinning out plums—how important this is. The leaves have been removed so that you can see the plums. See text for instructions.

AN ESPALIER TREE AFTER TRAINING

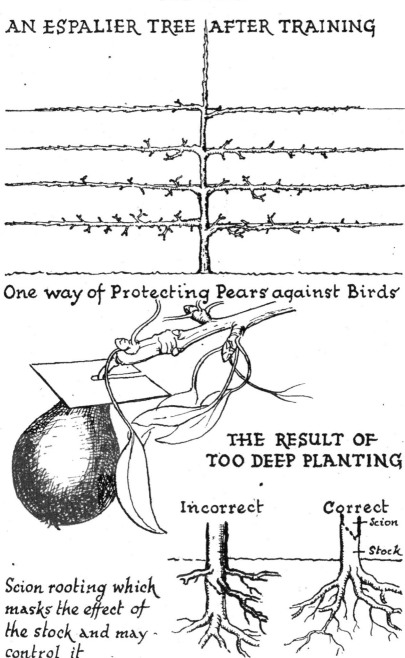

One way of Protecting Pears against Birds

THE RESULT OF TOO DEEP PLANTING

Incorrect

Correct

Scion

Stock

Scion rooting which
masks the effect of
the stock and may
control it

C

pears good drenchings with water during droughty periods in the summer when it is seen that the leaves are drooping somewhat. Much can be done to prevent such a condition if mulchings are applied around the stems of the trees for 3 or 4 ft. This consists of putting on the surface of the ground well-rotted compost, lawn mowings or damped horticultural peat at the rate of 1 really heaped bucketful per square yard. Before applying a mulch it is a good plan to hoe the ground lightly to break up any pan there may be.

When watering does have to be done it is invaluable to put on a mulch immediately afterwards so as to ensure retaining the water given off by preventing evaporation.

Thinning.—See that each pear has ample room to develop properly. This usually means having no fruit closer than 5 inches from the next. This is particularly important with varieties like Fertility and Hessle, which normally bear such tiny pears. In fact one can say that more severe thinning should be done in the case of varieties bearing small fruits than in the case of those naturally bearing larger specimens.

Fruit Protection.—You can prevent birds and wasps attacking pears by surrounding the individual fruits with muslin or paper bags tied on to the spur or branch. These also prevent the fruits from falling and getting bruised.

Flooding and Mulching.—When pears are grown against walls or fences or in enclosed gardens they often find it difficult to " hold " their crops in droughty summers. It is advisable, therefore, in late May or early June to fork the ground over shallowly so as to break up any pan that may have formed on the surface, and then to give a regular drenching with water. After the drenching, decaying organic matter should be applied around the trees for 3 or 4 ft. and to a depth of 2 or 3 inches, to provide a good mulch which will help to keep the moisture in the soil.

Sometimes a good mulching if applied at the beginning of June, will make it unnecessary to flood.

JOBS TO DO—MONTH BY MONTH

(a) *Winter Pruning.*—This should be carried out as early as possible directly the leaves have fallen, all the prunings being cleared up and burnt. Any large cuts made should be cleaned with a sharp knife and painted with a thick whitelead paint. November—December.

(b) *Winter Spraying.*—This is not always necessary in the case of pears, for it is seldom that pears are attacked by aphides, and so the tar oil spraying need only be necessary, say, once every five years. December.

(c) *Winter Digging.*—This should be carried out immediately after the prunings have been cleared up (for details see apples, page 44). November–December.

(d) *Manuring.*—As for apples (see page 31). December.

(e) *Nitrogen.*—It is seldom necessary to give pears extra nitrogen in January as it is in the case of apples. January.

(f) *Leaf Blister-Mite.*—Before the pre-blossom wash, though, it may be necessary to spray the trees with lime-sulphur 1 in 30 against the Pear-leaf Blister Mite, and this should be done during the month of February.

(g) *Lime Sulphur.*—Before and after blossoming. On the whole, pears are more susceptible to scab than apples, and thorough lime-sulphur sprayings are necessary. Use the Lime Sulphur at 1 in 30. April.

(h) *Nicotine and Arsenate of Lead.*—It may be necessary to spray with nicotine should aphides be present. The nicotine may be added to the lime-sulphur together with a " spreader "—like Estol H. Lead arsenate can be added to the lime-sulphur also, should caterpillars be doing damage. April.

(i) *Summer Cultivation.*—Regular hoeing, if on cultivated land, throughout the summer until the end of June.

(j) Summer pruning during the months of June, July and August.

(k) *Pear Midge Removal.*—The removal of any fruits seen to be affected by pear midge. May—June.

(l) *Thinning.* Most varieties of pears pay for thinning, though there is certainly one variety, Conference, which may be left alone. No pear should be left closer than 5 inches on any one branch. It is always better to thin pears with scissors than with the thumb and forefinger. Early July.

(*m*) *Staving.*—Branches of pears, when they are cropping heavily, particularly varieties such as William's or Conference, are apt to break, and it may be necessary to " stave " them up in some way. This may be done by driving a pole into the ground and tying a branch up to this, or by tying the pole in the centre of the tree and attaching the branches to the top of the pole like strings to a maypole. July—August.

(*o*) *Wasps and Birds.*—Birds and wasps will go for pears as they are ripening and will often attack them long before they are fit to pick. Individual fruits may be protected by tying around them muslin or paper bags. If these are tied to the spur or the branch it ensures that if the fruit should fall it will not get damaged. The drawing shows how cards can be used to protect pears from bird pecking. The slit may easily be made with a pair of scissors. See page 65.

(*p*) *Harvesting and Storing.*—Growers should not only learn to pick pears at the right time, but also to recognise varieties which will not keep. The chart on page 71 gives the season the pears can be used quite clearly. They will go " sleepy " almost overnight.

Mealiness in pears is a sign that the fruits have been left too long on the trees. Pick the early and mid season varieties before the green " base " colour has turned yellow. Varieties like Dr. Jules Guyot have to be picked quite green, while the " russetty " and reddish tinge types like William's and Clapp's Favourite may have a little of their natural colour present ; but again the base of the colour must be green and not lemon.

A simple test is to lift the pear in the palm of the hand and if when it gets to the horizontal it comes away from the spur naturally—it is ready. Generally speaking the earlies are picked in late July or early August—depending on the location and season. " Mids " will be picked 3 weeks or so later.

Pears should always be stored separately from apples if possible. Oiled paper wraps should not be used for pears that are going to be stored for any length of time. Normally

THE PEAR

pears need a storage temperature of from 40° to 45° F. Store in trays and do not let the fruits touch one another.

VARIETIES (in order of maturing).

THREE VARIETIES FOR TINY GARDEN :
*Conference.   Dr. Jules Goyot.
Laxton's Superb.
* Choose this if you only plant one.

SELECTED LIST FOR SMALL GARDEN :

Eaters.	Cookers.
Laxton's Super b.	Catillac.
William's Bon Chrêtien.	Uvedale's St. Germain.
Marie Louise.	
Conference.	
Doyenne du Comice.	
Durondeau.	
Josephine de Malines.	

VARIETIES FOR STANDARDS OR HALF STANDARDS :

William's Bon Chrêtien.	Emile d'Heyst.
Souvenir de Congrés.	Hessle.
Jargonelle.	Doyenne du Comice.
Louise Bonne de Jersey.	Beurré Diel.

VARIETIES THAT WILL EAT OR COOK :

Beurré Capiaumont.	Durondeau.
William's.	Beurré Diel.
Pitmaston Duchess.	

FOR THE EPICURE :

Eaters.

William's Bon Chrêtien.	Marie Louise.
Beurré Superfin.	Doyenne du Comice.
Comte de Lamy.	Glou Morceau.
Thompson's.	Duchesse de Bôrdeaux.

TWELVE GOOD DESSERTS IN ORDER OF RIPENING :

Clapp's Favourite.	Beurre Hardy.
Dr. Jules Guyot.	Conference.
Laxton's Superb.	Thompson's.
William's Bon Chrêtien.	Durondeau.
Marguerite Marillat.	Doyenne du Comice.
Beurre Superfin.	Winter Nelis.

113

DESSERT VARIETIES FOR CORDONS OR ESPALIERS FOR SUCCESSION :

Doyenne d'Eté . . .	July.
Laxton's Superb . . .	August.
William's Bon Chrêtien .	August.
Souvenir de Congrès . .	September.
Dr. Jules Guyot . . .	September.
Conference	October—November.
Durondeau	October—November.
Emile d'Heyst . . .	October—November.
Beurré Hardy . . .	October.
Doyenne du Comice . .	October.
Charles Ernest . . .	November.
Fondant de Thirriot . .	November—December.
Josephine de Malines .	January.

PEARS

Variety.	Cooker or Eater	When to Pick.	Habit of Growth.	When to Use.	Remarks.
Beurré d'Amanlis	E	About Aug. 30th	Vigorous Spreading.	Sept. (early).	Good cropper. Very juicy. Medium to large. Pleasant flavour. Used for double working. Good for Midlands and North.
Beurré de Capiaumont	E	About Sept. 21st	Slightly spreading, moderate.	October.	Regular cropper. Fruit cooks well. Medium size, good colour. Brownish red flush. Hardy.
Beurré Diel	E	About Sept. 1st	Upright, strong.	Oct.–Nov.	An excellent cropper. Fruit large, rough, yellow. Quality excellent when well ripened. Prune hard. Likes a warm sheltered site.
Beurré Hardy	E	About Sept. 24th	Upright, very strong.	October.	Shy cropper. Fruit large, brown, red flush. Quality good. Hardy. Gather fruit before ripe.
Beurré Superfin	E	About Sept. 14th	Slightly spreading, strong.	October.	Medium cropper. Fruit medium, yellow, finely russeted. Quality excellent. Needs watching in store. Pick early and eat while firm. Early flowering.
Catillac	C	About Oct. 21st	Spreading, strong.	Feb.–April.	A regular cropper. Fruit large, green, reddish flush. Quality as stewing pear excellent. Mid-season flowering. Prune lightly.
Charles Ernest	E	About Oct. 14th	Upright, strong.	Oct.–Nov.	Excellent cropper. Fruit large, yellow, scarlet flesh. Quality good. Delicate flavour. Good for top grafting.
Clapp's Favourite		About Aug. 25th	Medium grower.	September.	Should be picked before it ripens as it does not keep. Light yellow fruit, red or bronze cheek, good flavour.

PEARS—*continued*

Variety.	Cooker or Eater	When to Pick.	Colour and Quality.	Habit of Growth.	Remarks.
Comte de Lamy	E	About Sept. 18th	Spreading, moderate.	Oct.–Nov.	Good cropper. Fruit small, pale green to yellow. Excellent flavour and quality. Likes a warm wall.
Conference	E	About Sept. 30th	Upright, slightly spreading, medium.	Oct.–Nov.	A regular, heavy cropper. Resists scab. Fruit large to medium. Green to yellow, spotted russeting. Flavour sweet and juicy. Good pollinator for most second early flowering varieties.
Doyenne du Comice	E	About Oct. 1st	Upright, spreading, medium.	November.	Crops irregularly. Corresponds to Cox's Orange Pippin in apples. Requires warm, well-drained soil. Quality excellent. Fruit large, yellow, red flush. Delicious flavour. Must have a pollinator, Glou Morceau or Laxton's Superb.
Doyenne d'Eté	E	About July 21st	Upright, spreading, weak.	July–Aug.	A good cropper. Fruit small, yellow, red-brown flush. Quality good. Excellent early variety.
Dr. Jules Guyot	E	About Aug. 21st	Upright, close, medium.	Sept. (early).	A good, heavy cropper. Fruit light yellow, pale-red flush. Quality moderate. Flavour distinct. Stores better when picked prior to full ripening.
Duchesse de Bordeaux	E	About Oct. 14th	Upright, large, moderate, slow.	Jan.–March.	Medium cropper. Fruit medium, yellow, russeted with rough red. Keeps well. Flavour and quality excellent.
Durondeau	E	About Sept. 30th	Upright, close, medium.	Oct.–Nov.	Excellent cropper. Fruit large, long, yellow, with gold and red russet. Quality and flavour good when well grown.

PEARS—continued

Variety.	Cooker or Eater	When to Pick.	Habit of Growth.	When to Use.	Remarks.
Emile d'Heyst	E	About Sept. 30th	Dwarfish, spreading, as standard, medium.	Oct.–Nov.	Regular cropper. Fruit medium, light yellow, brown russet. Quality good. with aromatic flavour. Leaves crimson in autumn. Distinctly hardy.
Fondant de Thirriot	E	About Sept. 1st	Upright, vigorous.	Sept.–Oct.	Outstanding cropper. Fruit large, pale yellow, dull red flush. Flavour best on warm soils.
Glou Morceau	E	About Oct. 14th	Spreading, strong.	Dec.–Feb.	Good cropper. Fruit medium, green, ripens yellow. A good keeping variety, ripening successionally when stored.
Hessle	E	About Sept. 21st	Upright, spreading, vigorous.	October.	Regular, heavy cropper. Fruit small, brown to yellow, russet dots. Quality moderate. Flavour sweet and juicy. Hardy.
Jargonelle	E	About Aug. 1st	Untidy, vigorous.	August.	Heavy cropper. Fruit medium long, yellow-green, red flush. Quality tender and juicy. Needs picking before quite ripe. Soon decays. Good flavour.
Josephine de Malines	E	About Oct. 1st	Spreading, moderate.	Dec.–Jan.	Regular, good cropper. Fruit smallish, light greenish yellow. Delicious flavour and excellent quality. Tip bearer. A reliable keeping variety.
Laxton's Superb	E	About Aug. 30th	Upright, spreading, moderate.	Sept. (early).	Good cropper. Larger than Beurré Superfin. Quality good. Flavour sweet, juicy.
Louise Bonne de Jersey	E	About Sept. 21st	Spreading, upright, medium.	October.	Regular, heavy cropper. Fruit medium green-yellow, red spots and flush. Quality very good. Flavour good, sweet.

117

Variety.	Cooker or Eater	When to Pick.	Habit of Growth.	When to Use.	Remarks.
Marie Louise	E	About Sept. 21st	Untidy, spreading, medium growth.	Oct.–Nov.	Good cropper, irregular at times. Fruit medium light green to yellow. Quality good. Flavour characteristic.
Pitmaston Duchess	CE	About Sept. 30th	Upright, spreading, very vigorous.	Oct.–Nov.	Regular cropper. Susceptible to scab. Fruit very large. Yellow, russeted. Quality good. Flavour good when well grown and season good.
Roosevelt	E	About Sept. 30th	Upright, strong, compact.	Oct.–Nov.	A good cropper. Fruit very large, yellow, distinct red flush and dots. Quality medium. Flavour good in good season.
Souvenir de Congres	E	About Sept. 1st	Upright, spreading, compact, medium.	September.	Slightly irregular cropping, but good Fruit large, yellow, red cheek, striped russet. Quality good. Flavour very sweet, musky.
Thompson's	E	About Sept. 21st	Upright, spreading, medium.	Oct.–Nov.	Moderate cropper. Fruit fairly large, yellow, russeted. Quality good, delicious flavour.
Uvedale's St. Germain	C	About Sept. 30th	Upright, very strong.	Oct.–March.	A moderate cropper. Fruit extremely large, green, black dots. Quality very moderate.
Vicar of Winkfield	C	About Sept. 30th	Moderate grower.	Nov.–Jan.	Prune lightly. Bright green fruit, turning yellow. Can be used for dessert. Hardy and prolific.
William's Bon Chretien	EC	About Aug. 30th	Slightly spreading, moderate.	September.	A good regular cropper. Fruit large yellow, faint red stripe, slightly russeted. Quality good. Flavour has strong musky quality. Juicy, sweet. Gather green and ripen in store.

N.B.—Most dessert pears if gathered when hard and green, cook quite well.

118

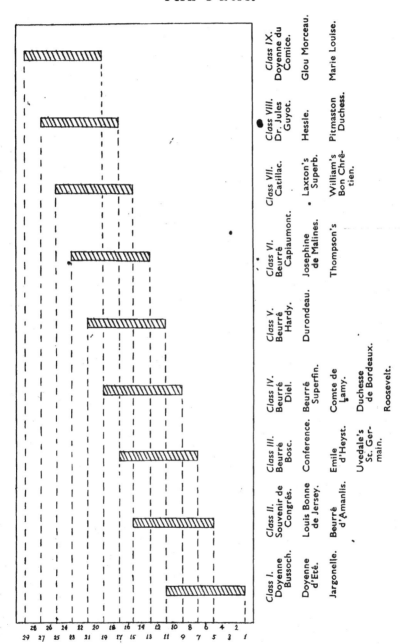

PEARS—Periods in which flowering may be expected

Class I. Doyenne Bussoch.	Class II. Souvenir de Congrès.	Class III. Beurré Bosc.	Class IV. Beurré Diel.	Class V. Beurré Hardy.	Class VI. Beurré Capiaumont.	Class VII. Catillac.	Class VIII. Dr. Jules Guyot.	Class IX. Doyenne du Comice.
Doyenne d'Eté.	Louis Bonne de Jersey.	Conference.	Beurré Superfin.	Durondeau.	Josephine de Malines.	Laxton's Superb.	Hessle.	Glou Morceau.
Jargonelle.	Beurré d'Amanlis.	Emile d'Heyst.	Comte de Lamy.		Thompson's	William's Bon Chrétien.	Pitmaston Duchess.	Marie Louise.
		Uvedale's St. Germain.	Duchesse de Bordeaux.					
			Roosevelt.					

119

THE PEAR

The oldest deciduous fruit trees in California are pear trees, as has already been stated in the account of fruits at the old missions, and some of the trees are still bearing, though it is about a century and a half since their planting. Trees planted by pioneers in the old mining districts have actually assumed semblance to adjacent oaks, Notable instances are found in the Stillwater district of Shasta County and elsewhere. Near San Jose there is a tree over half a century old, with a trunk seven and a half feet around and yielding annually about fifteen hundred pounds of fruit, some of which was exhibited at the Columbian Exposition.

The pear withstands neglect and thrives in soils and situations which other fruit trees would rebel against. It defies drouth and excessive moisture, and patiently proceeds with its fruitage even when the soil is trampel almost to rocky hardness by cattle, carrying its fruit and foliage aloft above their reach. And yet the pear repays care and good treatment, and receives them from California growers, for the pear has been one of our most profitable fruits. It is in demand for canning, for drying, and for distant shipment, and its long season and the slow ripening after picking allow deliberation in marketing, and admit of enjoying low rates for shipment by slow trains. One of the most striking demonstrations of the commercial suitability of the California pear is found in successful marketing in London. Solomons, who was called "London's greatest fruiterer," said in 1903 that California Bartletts from Block of Santa Clara are the "best in the world." Even after crossing the continent they seemed to endure shipment across the Atlantic better than Eastern pears.

The most obvious marks of the California pear are size and beauty. The most conspicuous example is the Bartlett, which is the pear of California, judged by its popularity, fresh, canned and dried. When well grown, its size is grand, and its delicate color, aroma and richness unsurpassed. What extreme in point of size has been reached is not known to the writer, but he saw at the San Jose Horticultural Fair, of 1886, thirteen Bartlett pears grown by A. Block, of Santa Clara, which weighed fourteen pounds, the heaviest of the group weighing twenty-two and one-half ounces. But there had been larger Bartletts than the writer then saw, for in 1858 a Bartlett was shown at Sacramento which weighed 27 ounces and was $13\frac{1}{4}$ inches in girth, and to meet incredulity a life-size outline of the fruit was published in the California Culturist of December, 1858. Other pears have made standard sizes in California far in advance of their records elsewhere. There was in 1870 a Pound pear sent from Sacramento to the late Marshall P. Wilder, president of the American Pomological Society, which weighed four pounds and nine ounces, and was reported by Colonel Wilder to be larger than anything previously reported in pear annals.* But California has recently done even better, for a pear from near Marysville in 1904 was reported as nine inches high, sixteen inches around the base and five pounds in weight. Notes kept by the writer include five Vicar of Winkfields weighing four pounds eight ounces; nine Easter Beurre weighing twenty-four and one-half pounds, the heaviest single specimen weighing two and three-fourths pounds; thirty-five Beurre Clairgeau weighing thirty-seven pounds, the heaviest one, nineteen ounces; Seckel pears, nine and three-fourths inches in circumference—Downing's figures make the Seckel five and seven-eighths inches around.

The pear comes into bearing early if conditions have favored the thrift and development of the tree. It is a long-lived tree as already shown unless it is invaded by the blight. It is the judgment of Hayward Reed, whose pear orchards in Sacramento and Yuba Counties have long been among the best known in California, that with variations due to climate, soil, drainage, variety, etc., a pear tree is mature at 12 to 15 years of age and will average eight or nine boxes of 50 pounds each. It will pay for its care at seven to ten years of age.

LOCALITIES FOR THE PEAR

The pear has a wider range than the apple in local adaptations. It does as well as the apple in the coast regions, if suitable varieties are grown; it thrives far better than the apple in the interior valleys; it rivals the apple in the ascent of the slope of the Sierra Nevada, and gains from the altitude, color and late keeping, as does the apple. By rejecting a few naturally tender varieties, or by proper protection against the scab fungus, in regions where its attacks are severe, one can grow pears almost everywhere in California—providing pear blight can be held in check, as will be discussed later.

The choice of location is governed more by commercial considerations than by natural phenomena. The same facts which make the Bartlett the favorite variety with planters, also should regulate the choice of locality for growing it. These facts were expressed by the late C. W. Reed, of Sacramento, who was in his time one of the leading pear growers and shippers of the State, as follows:

In the Sacramento Valley proper there is but one variety of pear that will justify extensive cultivation, viz., the Bartlett. While nearly all varieties may be grown successfully, and many varieties may be desirable for home purposes, yet for profitable orchards we have to confine ourselves to this one variety, except in high altitudes, or localities where the fruit only matures very late. The reason for this will be better understood by the inexperienced if explained. The Bartlett pear having qualities that make it a universal favorite for shipping, canning, and for domestic market, no other variety is wanted while it is obtainable. With the difference in the time of its ripening in different localities that are adjacent, our mar-

---

*Tilton's Journal of Horticulture, March, 1871, p. 87. An engraving of this fruit natural size, was given in the Pacific Rural Press, November 8, 1873."

kets are supplied with this variety about four months each season, viz., July, August, September and October. While this pear is in the market, any other variety to compete with it must sell at very low prices.

Of course experienced pear growers, whose taste would soon cloy with a continuous diet of Bartletts, and who know fully the superior quality of other varieties which ripen soon after it, would dispute the position taken by Mr. Reed, but for present California taste and trade he is undoubtedly correct. As the canners and shippers and local consumers all call for Bartletts, and as they usually sell at the East for more than other varieties, the choice of location to secure a Bartlett, either very early or very late, is the part of wisdom, for either end of the season usually yields better prices than the middle. The earliest Bartletts come from the interior valley sometimes as early as the last week in June; the next, from the valleys adjacent to the Bay of San Francisco; the next, from the higher foothills of the Sierra Nevada; and the last, so far as present experience goes, although some coast and mountain situations are quite late, reach the market from the Vacaville district. It is an interesting fact that this district, which has long been famous for marketing the first early fruits, should also market very late ones. It is true, however, that early fruits hasten to maturity and late fruits are retarded. Late fruits push along until about midsummer, then stop growing for a month or two during the hottest weather, and afterwards proceed on their course and finish up well.* W. W. Smith, of Vaca Valley, has picked Bartletts as late as November 19, but that is unusually late. In years with heavy late spring rains the Bartlett ripens earlier in the Vaca Valley than in ordinary seasons, and when the fruit sells well in the East, the Bartletts are gathered green and shipped all through the season, as their first growth usually makes them large enough for this purpose.

There is produced in some situations a "second crop" of Bartletts and of other varieties, which is of account when pears are scarce and is sometimes dried with profit. For such fruit the bloom appears upon the tips of the shoots of the current season's growth. The fruit is sometimes coreless and has led to claims of "seedless pears." Bartlett pears have actually been picked in the foothills above Peatz in Butte County on February 25, 1905, and described as "fine, delicious and ripe." This fact must be regarded as a token of local climatic salubrity and not of economic or pomological account.

Bartletts can also be successfully held in storage for a time if fitted for it. The experiments of the United States Department of Agriculture, conducted in Southern Oregon, show that the Bartlett season can be extended from six to seven weeks by leaving the fruit on the trees two weeks longer than is at present the practice and by storing for four or five weeks at a temperature of 32 deg. or 34 deg. F. after the fruit has been precooled.

---

*Demonstration of the effect of high heat in retarding the ripening of pears has been described by R. H. Taylor and E. L. Overholser in Monthly Bulletin California State Horticultural Commission for March, 1919.

SOILS FOR THE PEAR

The pear, if it is not allowed to dry out entirely, will generally do well on shallow soil and over a tight clay hard-pan, where most other fruits would be unsatisfactory or fail utterly. The trees will thrive in clay loams, and even in adobe, if properly cultivated. In laying out fruit farms, which often include a variety of soils, even in comparatively small area, the pears and plums (if on the right stock, as will be seen) should be set in the lower, moister, stiffer soil, and other fruits on the lighter, warmer, and better drained portions. The pear, however, enjoys the better situation, though it will thrive on the poorer. The tree seems to attain its greater growth and heavier bearing on the alluvial soils of the valleys and near the banks of rivers and streams. All pears will be later in maturing and have better keeping qualities if grown on a clay subsoil. Thus it appears that the pear will flourish whether the water is near or far from the surface. On wet land the apple is apt to die in a few years, or become worthless. On dry land the apple may live longer than on wet land, but the fruit will be small and tasteless. But the pear tree may bear good fruit, under both extreme conditions.

It has been learned by experience that the pear will flourish on soil somewhat alkaline. At the University Agricultural Experiment Station at Tulare, this subject was demonstrated in detail. It was shown that though the pear endures a certain amount of alkali its limit of endurance may be often exceeded and there is little warrant to select alkali soil for pears, unless it be to fill a space that would otherwise be vacent in the orchard. If it is not too alkaline the pears will thrive. If gypsum be used in planting, somewhat stronger alkali will be endured than otherwise.

PROPAGATION AND PLANTING

The use of dwarfing stock for the pear has been nearly abandoned in this State, though in early years the quince was largely used. The most prominent orchard on quince stock is that of A. Block, of Santa Clara, where may be seen dwarf trees originally planted eight feet apart in squares, but now wider spaced by removing part of the trees; the remainder doing exceedingly well under liberal manuring and irrigation. It would, however, require special investigation to determine whether these trees are still dependent upon the quince or whether they have developed roots from the pear wood above.

It is quite possibe that, at least for gardens, there may be in the future more use made of dwarf trees; but for commercial orchards there appears no need of dwarfing. The common conclusion is that it is better to have fewer trees and larger ones, but since the pear blight became an issue in this State the quince has been advocated as a means of maintaining a sound root and keeping the warfare above ground. The best known dwarf pear orchard of recent planting is that of the Hillgirt Orchards in the

◢

Alhambra Valley near Martinez in Contra Costa County. The reasons for resort to the quince root and the results are thus given by Mr. Frank T. Swett:

The Bartlett does not make good union with the quince root, but by working Beurre Hardy on the quince root, and Bartlett on the Hardy, perfect unions are obtained. We have a three-story pear tree:root, quince; stem to a height of 12 inches, Beurre Hardy; top, Bartlett. We had a commercial crop of a box to the tree, or 170 boxes to the acre at the sixth year. Since then, we have had five good crops of pears. Standard trees alongside are only just beginning to bear commercial crops. We have, therefore, had an income for five years which would not have come to us on this land with standard trees. In 1907 we picked 1200 boxes of fine, clean, shapely pears from three acres of dwarfs. Our trees are planted 16 feet apart. I think 14 feet apart would be a little better, giving 221 trees to the acre instead of 170. The trees are stocky and strong. They are from 6 to 8 inches in diameter a foot above the ground. They are about 10 to 12 feet high, and are broad and spreading.

There are some cultural advantages of the dwarf trees. Our men prune about 60 of these trees a day as against 16 to 20 standard trees. Spraying can be more thoroughly done, as the trees are close to the ground. Most of the pears are picked without the use of a ladder, and only a short ladder is required to gather the pears higher up. I have seen a good picker picking at the rate of 60 boxes a day on these dwarfs, where the average rate on standard trees was 20 boxes a day. We resorted to the quince root to escape the root aphis, but the quince root is not as resistant to oak fungus as the French root, and where this fungus is a menace, dwarfs should not be planted. Dwarf trees suffer just as severely from blight as standard trees.

The following varieties are commended for cultivation on quince stock as dwarfs, experience proving them vigorous growers and abundant bearers in suitable localities: Bartlett (by double working), Beurre Hardy, Doyenne du Comice, Duchess d'Angouleme, Glout Morceau, Pound, Beurre Diel, White Doyenne, Easter Beurre, Winter Nelis, P. Barry, Winter Bartlett.

Blight-Proof Roots.—But the pear is usually grown in California by budding or grafting on its own roots; that is upon pear seedlings. Formerly these were almost exclusively imported from France, but in 1918 more than three-fourths of the nursery trees were grown on Japanese stock, and in 1921 seedlings of European species are almost wholly abandoned. The seedlings of the Sand pear, of Asia (Pyrus serotina), are being demonstrated to be inferior to other Asiatic species which are being introduced and bid fair to become a main reliance. Very interesting pamphlets describing these new species were published in 1918 and in 1920 by Mr. A. L. Wisker of Grass Valley, California, who is commending the growing of ussuriensis seedlings to be top-grafted in the orchard after attaining some size.

It is, however, not demonstrated that these Asiatic species will be our only reliance in the future, for even if some of them do furnish a resistant root they may not make a good stem and, therefore, it is proposed to bud or graft some other resistant wood to make a trunk and top work the Bartlett upon such a trunk so that only the branches shall be susceptible to blight. Such a trunk is commended by Dr. W. L. Howard of the University of California in the use of the variety named "Surprise," whose resistance is demonstrated:

The Surprise is even more blight resistant than the Japanese pear and makes a beautiful tree, and the plan to follow would be to grow the Surprise on the Japanese root until the trees are perhaps four years old, or until all of the main scaffold branches have been formed. These may then be top-worked to Bartlett. In this way, even though blight did get into the trees, it would not be possible to lose more than one of the main branches, and if care were taken this could be again top-worked on the original Surprise stump.

Distance in Planting.—If the pears are to have the whole ground, it is usual to plant from twenty to twenty-four feet apart on the square. As the tree is slower to attain size and full bearing than the stone fruits, and as it is a long-lived tree, the pears are sometimes set twenty-four feet with plums in quincunx. Peaches and apricots are also set between pears sometimes, when the soil chosen for pears suits them also.

PRUNING

Usually the pear is grown in the vase form, as described in the general chapter on pruning. With regular, upright growers, heading low and cutting to outside buds results in a handsome, gently-spreading top, and effectually curbs the disposition which some varieties, notably the Bartlett, have to run straight up with main branches crowded together.

The development of the vase-form with a few continuous leaders, in a general way as prescribed for the peach in Chapter XX, is practicable. Such leaders are to be covered with short, fruit-bearing laterals. Thinning and shortening of laterals can be done by summer pruning.

As with other fruit trees, the pear must be studied and pruning must be done with an understanding of the habit of the variety under treatment. Irregular and wayward growers, which, in windy places, also have their rambling disposition promoted by prevailing winds, often give the grower much perplexity. The general rules of cutting to an outside bud to spread the tree, to an inside bud to raise and concentrate it, and to an outside bud one year and an inside bud the next, if a limb is desired to continue in a certain course, are all helpful to the pruner. But with some pears, of which the Winter Nelis is a conspicuous example, it is exceedingly hard to shape the tree by these general rules, and some growers abandon all rules, merely shortening in where too great extension is seen, or to facilitate cultivation, and trust to shaping the tree when it shall have finished its rampant growing period.

In the hot interior valleys, with the pear as with the apple, care must be taken to prune so as not to open the tree too much to the sun, but to shorten in and thin out only so far as is consistent with maintaining a good covering of foliage.

The pruning of bearing pear trees is much like that of the apple, to be determined largely by the habit of the tree, and to secure a fair amount of fruit on branches with strength and stiffness enough to sustain it.

Summer pruning will promote fruiting either in a young or an old tree and some practice it to secure early bearing of young trees, but the common practice is winter pruning to secure strong wood and prevent overbearing.

THINNING PEARS

It is quit important to attend to thinning the fruit on overloaded trees. Even the popular Bartlett will often give fruit too small for profitable sale unless thinned, though successive pickings as the fruit reaches marketable size, which will be commended presently, does to a degree reduce the danger of overcrowding. With pears, as other fruits, thinning should not be done until it is seen that the fruit is well set. Dropping off from natural causes sometimes thins the crop quite enough.

IRRIGATION OF THE PEAR

In some situations the pear needs irrigation, though it will endure drouth which would destroy most other fruit trees. There is no profit in small, tough fruit. As stated in the chapter on irrigation the wood growth and fruit show whether proper moisture needs are met or not. Early pears are advanced in development by irrigation in some parts of the State, and this is an important factor in their value. On the other hand, late pears may be kept growing to larger size and later maturity by irrigation. The following is an interesting concrete instance:

Mr. John McAlister of Santa Clara County got nearly double the price for his pears one year because he held them back from ripening by timely irrigation. The weather in August and September when the Bartletts and Beurre Hardys ripen is a little too warm to accomplish much by irrigation except to increase the size of the fruit. The Hardys were irrigated two weeks before picking early in September; and after they were picked, the Comice, Winter Neils, and Easter Beurre were irrigated. The Comice were picked just before the Neils and the Neils were three inches in diameter before they needed to be picked late in November. The Easter Beurres six weeks after the Hardys, which brought the picking up to January 1. The Easter Beurres were 3½, 4, and 6 inches in diameter at that time. The pears had been held on the trees at least a month later than other people, and some of them were held in storage until March 1 before shipping to the eastern and coast markets. The pears are right to pick when they are large enough and the seeds begin to turn brown; but this condition may be delayed and the size increased by late irrigation unless early rains are ample enough to produce the same effect.

BLIGHT OF THE PEAR

The pear blight appeared in the San Joaquin Valley about 1900. In 1904, after having nearly wiped out bearing trees in the southern counties of the San Joaquin Valley, the disease began to devastate the orchards along the Sacramento River through the vast area of rich valley land which it traverses and on which is situated our most extensive pear acreage. In 1905 resolute warfare was made upon the blight, with a large appropriation of State funds, by the plant disease experts of the United States Department of Agriculture and the California Agricultural Experiment Station, with the assistance of the local horticultural authorities. It was probably the greatest campaign ever made against a single tree disease, although some insect warfares have been greater. The outlines of the plans followed and the results attained are to be found in the publications of the institutions engaged.*

Detailed information concerning the treatment of blight as indicated by progressive research and experimentation is also to be had from these institutions and from California horticultural journals which record the latest methods and results by pear growers who are continually introducing new methods of applying the only treatment thus far found effective, and that is cutting out and burning the affected parts. The cutting must be below the parts seen to be diseased, even to the roots of the tree, and disinfecting the tools used in one cut before again cutting into the tree.†

It is usually best, unless one is thoroughly acquainted with the disease, to submit specimens of suspected blight to the University Experiment Station at Berkeley, for a beginner may be easily deceived. However, that the inexperienced person may have a general idea of what to look for, the following outline of symptoms is given:

The most obvious effect of blight to be seen during the growing season, is the blackening of the leaves and soft wood to which they are attached, as though these parts had been touched by a flame, and from this appearance comes its old common name, "fire-blight." More specifically, as Prof. R. E. Smith has written, the leaves, blossoms and young fruit wither and turn black on the affected portions but do not fall, remaining tightly attached to the twigs during the winter after the healthy leaves have fallen. The infection proceeds downwards through the inner bark of the twigs and branches, and when working vigorously the blight kills the twigs or whole branches very rapidly. The disease often runs down into the large limbs, where it remains alive over winter, producing the so-called "holdover" blight, which is a source of infection during the following season.

The blighted twigs, branches or trunks show a red, sappy, juicy condition of the inner bark when infected with the true pear blight organism. If the disease is fresh and active the bark when cut into is very juicy, exuding the slightly sticky sap quite freely and showing bright red color in the inner bark. This symptom is of importance in distinguishing true blight from such troubles as die-back from sour sap, crater blight and other causes.

In the smaller twigs and branches the organism dries out and becomes entirely dead. But, through the agency of biting insects in the young shoots and suckers, the disease frequently gets into the trunk of the tree and also down into the roots. Here it spreads and causes the death of

*Reports of the California Commissioners of Horticulture, 1901 to 1906, including Reports on California Fruit Growers' Convention for 1905-6-7, Horticultural Commissioner, Sacramento. Report of Plant Pathologist, University Experiment Station, Berkeley, 1906 and 1908.

†The character of such a fight and what it costs is graphically portrayed by E. A. Gammon in the Report of California Fruit Growers' Convention of 1909, and in Pacific Rural Press, June 22, 1910.

the tree by slow degrees, due to the destruction of the inner bark of the trunk or main roots. In such cases the leaves of affected trees take on a peculiar bronzy reddish coloration in the fall, which is quite characteristic to the experienced eye.

From the "hold-over" blight in the trunks and large limbs an infectious sap exudes when growth starts in the spring, which sap contains myriads of the blight organisms. This sap is attractive to insects, which, in feeding upon it, get the blight bacteria upon their bodies and mouth parts, and transfer them to the blossoms or green shoots of other trees, thus spreading the infection.

Looking for Blight.—The time to see blight best is while the tree is in leaf. Discovery and cutting out should be in mind all summer—especially should thorough work be done in the autumn. The leaves are still hanging on blighted twigs; trees are least susceptible to reinfection from careless cutting because they are practically dormant; insects are not so numerous, and the rain is not yet soaking newly cut surfaces with drippings from other new cuts. It is easy to get around the orchard, and mud does not hinder following root blight.

Cutting Out Blight.—Cuts should usually be made about a foot below visible appearances of blight on the bark; (2) tools are disinfected before making the cut; (3) the wound immediately after the cutting is sponged with a disinfectant—of which the one chiefly used is one part of corrosive sublimate to 1000 parts of water by weight; which is one ordinary tablet of corrosive to one pint of water. Dr. F. C. Reimer of Oregon, the noted pear expert, recommends cyanide of mercury to disinfect cuts and wounds instead of corrosive sublimate—1 gram of pure cyanide of mercury to 500 grams of water (about one pint). Large cut surfaces should be subsequently brushed or sprayed with Bordeaux mixture or lime-sulphur wash.

Scraping Instead of Cutting.—In 1921 a new method of checking the progress of the blight downward is being employed in the treatment of larger branches and trunk. It is described as follows:*

The new method of control consists in the scraping of the outer layer of bark on all infected areas, and it is very essential to scrape for insurance at least eight to ten inches above and below all visible signs of blight. The scraped area is then painted or saturated with a solution of cyanide of mercury (1 to 500). On trunk infections it is found best to scrape a little closer to the cambium or growing layer of bark. It is found that the cyanide solution does not penetrate to the cambium if too much outer bark is left. On working on large areas disinfecting should be done several times during the operation because the surface of the bark becomes dry and the solution cannot penetrate to the inner blight. If a mud paste of cyanide solution and earth is put on the scraped area it helps to keep the wound damp for some time and the cyanide effective for a longer period. Bichloride solution, 1 to 1000, is better to use to disinfect tools. The bichloride solution and cyanide solution (1 to 500) may be mixed in the same bottle for convenience.

Pear Scab.—The scab fungus which seriously affects some varieties, and notably the Winter Nelis, is identical with the scab of the apple and will be mentioned in the chapter on tree disease.

---

*E. I. Power in Pacific Rural Press, March 26, 1921.

INSECT PESTS OF THE PEAR

The pear is subject to several grievous pests which must be resolutely combated or circumvented as described in Chapter XLI—where the identification of the pests is determined by the character of the injury they inflict.

GATHERING AND RIPENING OF PEARS

Many pear growers make the common mistake of allowing the fruit to hang too long on the tree, instead of gathering and ripening in a cool, dark place. Pears should be picked at the first indication of ripeness, the first sign being a tendency of the stem to part from the spur when the pear is gently raised up. This test applies especially to the Bartlett. Picking at this stage and laying away in the dark ripens up the Bartlett well. When picked at this stage and sent overland by slow freight, they ripen en route and the boxes open well on the Eastern markets. There are a few varieties which shrivel if ripened under cover, but the rule is a good one, and the grower will soon note the exceptions. Many desirable varieties have, no doubt, been pronounced poor and insipid because allowed to ripen on the tree. As a rule pears are ready to pick when of proper size, seeds beginning to turn brown, and the flesh quite firm.

Some pears size up and ripen before others. Some get oversized before the general run are ready. If these early pears are picked first, with some care not to knock the others off, the small ones left will have all the strength of the tree to increase their size, and the earliest ones will not get oversized or over-ripe. Fewer pickers are required and the job, being longer, is more attractive.

To ripen well, pears should be packed in tight boxes or inclosed in drawers. They do not do as well as apples on shelves open to circulation of air. As already stated, the oily-skinned apple endures exposure and maintains a smooth, ruddy cheek and sound heart in spite of wind, rain and rough weather. The pear under similar conditions decays rapidly.

POLLINATION OF PEARS

As very few varieties of pears are largely grown in California and as the Bartlett generally bears well when grown in large acreages by itself, the Eastern claim that the Bartlett is self-sterile does not seem to be justified in California experience. Recent observations indicate that even at the East the Bartlett is self-fertile when conditions are favorable to setting of the fruit and self-sterile when they are otherwise. As conditions are usually favorable in California this may be the reason why its self-fertility is more conspicuous here than at the East.

The behavior of the Bartlett under systematic fertilization has been determined at the University Farm at Davis and the results published in detail.* The conclusions are that the Bartlett is to a

---

*"Pollination of the Bartlett Pear," by W. P. Tufts, University of California Experiment Station, Bulletin No. 37; May, 1919.

limited degree self-sterile (and in 1920 was sterile) under valley conditions and is self-sterile under foothill conditions; therefore, it is desirable that another variety should be interplanted with the Bartlett for cross-pollination. The blooming season of eight varieties during a period of five years at Davis is given as follows:

Angouleme	March 16 to March 28
Howell	March 16 to March 29
Easter	March 16 to March 30
Clairgeau	March 22 to March 28
Comice	March 29 to March 31
Dana's Honey	March 23 to March 31
Winter Nelis	March 22 to April 2
Bartlett	March 19 to April 13

It thus appears that the Bartlett has a very long blooming season and overlaps the other varieties named—all of which were demonstrated by hand tests to be capable of cross-pollinating it and to receive the same service.

VARIETIES OF THE PEAR

Though large collections of famous Eastern and European pears have been brought to California, the peculiarity of the local market and demand for canning and shipping has led to concentration upon very few sorts.* The pears favorably considered by the 1920 conferences of growers, canners and nurserymen for commercial planting are the following: Bartlett, Beurre Bosc, Beurre Clairgeau, Beurre d'Anjou, Beurre Hardy, Comet, Easter Beurre, Forelle, Glout Morceau, Wilder, Winter Nelis, Comice.

The following descriptive list, arranged approximately in the order of their ripening includes varieties chiefly found in California orchards:

Harvest; syn. Sugar Pear (American).—Small, roundish, pale yellow, brownish in sun, brown and green dots; flesh, whitish, rather dry but sweet; tree upright, young wood olive yellow brown.

Madeleine (French).—Medium, obovate pyriform, stalk long and slender, set on the side of a small swelling; pale yellowish green, rarely brownish blush; calyx small, in shallow, furrowed basin; flesh white, juicy, delicate.

Wilder Early (American).—Small to medium, yellow with red cheek; sweet, and good. Recently introduced and profitable for local sale in San Diego County. Should not be confused with Col. Wilder, a California seedling which has gone out of use.

Bloodgood (New York).—Tree short, jointed, deep reddish brown wood; fruit medium turbinate, inclining to obovate, thickening abruptly in stalk; yellow, sprinkled with russet dots; calyx strong, open almost without depression; stalk obliquely inserted, without depression, short, fleshy at its base; flesh yellowish white, melting, sugary, aromatic; core small.

Clapp's Favorite (Massachusetts).—Tree a strong grower; young shoots dark reddish brown; fruit large, slightly obtuse pyriform; pale lemon yellow with brown dots; flesh fine, melting, juicy, with rich, sweet delicate, vinous flavor; resembles Bartlett, but lacks musky flavor.

---

*An illustrated account of the pears chiefly grown in California and cultural matters also, is given in an excellent publication by George P. Weldon on "Pear Culture in California," published in 1918 by the State Horticultural Commission, Sacramento.

Lawson; syn. Comet (New York).—Medium to large, bright crimson on yellow ground; flesh fine, rich and sweet; gaining in popularity.

Bartlett (English).—Tree a strong grower, early bearer, and healthy; fruit large, smooth, clear yellow, sometimes with delicate blush; stalk moderately long; stout and inserted in shallow cavity; calyx open; flesh white, fine grained, juicy, buttery; highly perfumed (musky), vinous flavor.

Buerre Hardy.—Large, long, obovate, sometimes obscurely pyriform; skin greenish with thin, brown russet; stalk an inch long; cavity small, uneven, oblique, basin shallow; buttery, somewhat melting, rich, slightly subacid; tree a strong grower.

Flemish Beauty (Belgian).—Large, obovate, often obscurely tapering to the crown, very obtuse, surface slightly rough, with some reddish brown russet on pale yellow ground; flesh juicy, melting, and good if picked early and ripened in the house; rejected commercially.

Seckel (Pennsylvania).—Rather small, ; regularly formed, obovate; brownish green, becoming yellowish brown, with russet red cheek; stalk slightly curved, and set in strifling depression; calyx small and set in a very slight depression; flesh whitish, buttery, very juicy and mélting, with peculiarly rich, spicy flavor and aroma. Only commended for home orchards.

Howell (Connecticut).—Rather large, roundish pyriform, light waxen yellow, often with finely-shaded cheek thickly sprinkled with minute russet dots and some russet patches; stalk medium, without cavity and sometimes lipped; sometimes in small cavity; calyx open in large, uneven basin; flesh whitish, juicy, brisk, vinous; not desirable commercially.

Duchess d'Angouleme (France).—Very large, oblong obovate; somewhat uneven, knobby surface; dull greenish yellow, streaked and spotted with russet; stalk long, stout, bent, deeply set in irregular cavity; calyx set in somewhat knobby basin; flesh white, buttery, and juicy, with rich flavor.

Louise Bonne of Jersey (France).—Large oblong pyriform, a little one-sided; glassy, pale green in shade, brownish red in the sun, numerous gray dots; stalk curved, rather obliquely inserted, without depression, or with a fleshy, enlarged base; calyx open in a shallow uneven basin; flesh very juicy, and melting, rich, and excellent; very prolific.

Beurre Bosc (Belgium).—Large pyriform, a little uneven, often tapering long and gradually into the stalk; skin pretty smooth, dark yellow, dots and streaks of cinnamon russet, slightly red on one side; stalk long, rather slender, curved; calyx short, in shallow basin; flesh white, melting, buttery, rich, with slightly perfumed flavor. Gaining commercial favor.

Beurre Clairgeau (France).—Large, pyriform, but with unequal sides; yellow, shaded with orange and crimson, thickly covered with russet dots, sometimes sprinkled with russet; stalk short, stout and fleshy, inserted by a lip at an inclination almost without depression; when lip is absent, the cavity is uneven; calyx open; flesh yellowish, buttery; juicy, granular, sugary, perfumed, vinous; apt to ripen early for a winter pear; good commercially.

Beurre d'Anjou (France).—Large, obtuse pyriform; stem, short, thick, and fleshy, in a cavity, surrounded by russet; calyx small, open in small cavity, russetted; skin greenish, sprinkled with russet, sometimes shaded with dull crimson, brown and crimson dots; flesh whitish, not very fine, melting, juicy, vinous flavor, perfumed; tree a fair grower, but somewhat affected by fungus; approved commercially.

Dana's Hovey; syn. Winter Seckel (Massachusetts).—Small, obovate, obtuse pyriform; greenish yellow or pale yellow, with much russet and brown dots; stalks rather short; a little curved, set in slight cavity, sometimes lipped; calyx open and basin small; flesh, yellowish, juicy, melting, sweet, aromatic; commended for home use.

Doyenne du Comice (France).—Large, varying, roundish pyriform, or broad, obtuse pyriform; greenish yellow becoming fine yellow, shaded with crimson, slightly marked with russet spots, and thickly sprinkled with russet dots; stalks short, stout, inclined and set in shallow cavity, often russetted; calyx small, open, basin large, deep and uneven; flesh white, fine, melting, aromatic. Very profitable during last few years in eastern shipments.

Glout Morceau (Flemish).—Rather large, varying in form, but usually short pyriform, approaching obtuse oval; neck very short and obtuse; body large and tapering towards crown; often considerably ribbed; green, becoming pale greenish yellow; stalk stout, moderately sunk; calyx large, basin distinct, rather irregular; flesh white, fine-grained, buttery, melting, rich, sweet, and fine flavor.

Block's Acme (California seedling, by A. Block, of Santa Clara).—Large and very handsome, surpassing Beurre Clairgeau in size and color; regularly formed, pyriform, skin pale yellow, covered with russet all over, which becomes a fine glowing red on the side exposed to the sun; flesh white, crisp, and melting, juicy, sweet and slightly musky.

Winter Nelis (Belgium).—Medium, roundish, obovate, narrowed in near the stalk; yellowish green, dotted with gray russet and a good deal covered with russet; stalk rather long, bent, and set in narrow cavity; calyx open in shallow basin; flesh yellowish white, fine grained, buttery, very melting, and full of rich, sweet, aromatic juice; an old standard late pear.

Forelle.—Medium size, handsome, greenish yellow; brilliant red cheek with brown spots; quality good; often very profitable for shipping, but not a free bearer.

P. Barry (California seedling, by B. S. Fox).—Fruit large, elongated pyriform, a little obtuse; skin deep yellow, nearly covered with a rich golden russet; stalk of medium length and thickness, set rather obliquely on a medium cavity, sometimes by a lip; flesh whitish, fine, juicy, melting, sweet, slightly vinous and rich. Not justifying expectations commercially.

Easter Beurre (France).—Large, roundish, obovate obtuse, often rather square in figure; yellowish green, sprinkled with many russet dots and some russet patches; stalk rather short, stout, set in an abruptly sunken obtuse cavity; calyx small, closed, but little snug among plaited folds of angular basin; flesh white, fine grained, very buttery, melting, and juicy, sweet, rich flavor; was successfully shipped from California to England as early as 1872 and retains favor for distant shipments.

Pound.—Large, pyriform, yellowish-green with red cheek, esteemed for cooking; reaches enormous size in this State, as already noted.

Kieffer and Le Conte.—These pears are grown to a limited extent in all parts of the State, but are usually condemned as inferior to the European varieties. The Kieffer is best in interior regions.

Crocker's Bartlett (California).—Chance seedling on place of L. L. Crocker, Loomis, Placer County. Introduced by Mr. Crocker in 1902. Described in year book, 1905, of U. S. Department of Agriculture; medium to large, oblong, obovate, pyriform; rich golden yellow, somewhat russetty; quality very good; keeps until March. Claimed to be blight-resistant and regularly productive, but has never gained much favor.

Winter Bartlett (Oregon).—Chance seedling in the dooryard of D. W. Coolidge in Eugene, Oregon. Closely resembles Bartlett in shape and appearance and flavor but coarser; ripens four months later than Bartlett in interior situations in California. Abandoned by some growers for coarseness, and disliked by canners for developing a pink color. Commercially disappointing.

PEARS

JOHN SCOTT, a famous Somersetshire nurseryman around 1870, whose firm still survives, had a collection of eighteen hundred different varieties of Pear, both eating and cooking. To-day his firm list no more than thirty-six. He gave it as his opinion that in France no less than two thousand varieties of Perry pear alone existed. Although these were the spacious days of gardening when great industrialists and landowners vied with each other in their collection it is probable that a good many pear varieties varied in little more than name.

In the old days the West of England was a great district for pear and apple growing, for in the sixteenth century both cider and perry making were considerable industries; indeed the gradual decline in their popularity began only after the Napoleonic wars, when the Continental wines and brandy became favoured. Before then both cider and perry were "exported" in bulk from Worcestershire to London and the North and were deservedly popular.

At that time, no doubt, many notable vintages existed. To-day, while cider is still popular enough to justify a production of over twenty million gallons, perry has almost disappeared, though just occasionally the visitor to out-of-the-way farms in the West may find himself drinking a delectable perry with a bouquet and flavour as rare as that of a fine hock. Usually, however, after the first sip of a proffered perry he longs for a handy pot-plant on which to tip the remains of the nauseous concoction while his host's back is turned.

Though the public demand for perry has declined some wonderful old pear trees are still to be seen in the West Midlands, towering skywards, white with blossom in spring and blazing bonfires of gold and crimson leaf in autumn. The Barland Pear, a famous variety, can still be identified by the twist in the lines of its stem bark. Most of the old pears were raised on pear stock grown from the pips, but in some farm orchards less vigorous specimens can still be seen with a sucker or two of the hawthorn rising from their bases, for our great-grandfathers liked the hawthorn well enough as a stock for medlars, pears and apples.

Pips from perry making provided stocks with some variation in strength though usually they inclined to the vigorous. Many elderly garden trees, both on walls and in the open, were worked on stocks of this type and grew far too strongly to combine fruitfulness with the stiff and restricted shape demanded by the old-time gardeners. The masses of strong but sappy shoots resulting from over-hard pruning rendered them extremely susceptible to scab attacks and for this reason the pear has gained the reputation of being rather a difficult fruit to grow.

Though pears are afflicted by fewer pests and fungi than apples there are very few varieties which can be expected to stand complete neglect. Since the whole aim and object of this book is to induce the amateur to go to the trouble of spraying and looking after all his fruit I do not propose to name them. It is because of neglect that it is unusual to find pears doing well in the small garden. Scab, and its boon companion canker, will soon destroy or mutilate trees of most varieties unless they are maintained in healthy condition by regular lime-sulphur or bordeaux spraying. Usually the survivors of neglect are large trees worked on the seedling stocks, where dead wood and growth replacement are about equal. Pitmaston Duchess may be cited as a typical variety and Williams Bon Chrétien (plain Williams to most people) is another. Immense numbers of Williams pears exist and though their cropping power is good, the fruit they produce under neglected conditions is scabby and fit only for the lowest type of trade.

Where pear trees are happy in their rooting and site it is

common to find good crops of clean fruit arriving with little or no attention until along comes a soaking summer and the fair faces of the fruits are marred with scab and wood infection is left for next year. Where trees are more or less left to their own devices maturity and slowed growth may also make them resistant to disease and fine trees of Jargonelle, Marie Louise, Emile d'Heyst, Louise Bonne of Jersey and Vicar of Winkfield have been noted by the author in past years, but always on soils which suited them. Pear trees grown on walls, sunny walls in particular, are much less afflicted by scab than trees in the open. This is to be expected, for they get less rain and wind and enjoy that little bit of added warmth which must remind them of the European summer enjoyed by their ancestors. Wall pears will crop if properly managed and planted with due regard to the Fruit Fertility Rules (see p. 120). Summer pruning is an essential factor in presuading strong-growing wall pears to carry heavy crops and at times root pruning is equally necessary.

Soil and Site.

The choicest pears are grown on a deep, warm, moisture-holding soil, but most pears are no more particular in their soil requirements than apples. For commercial success save in a few varieties this rules out the light, sandy or shallow soils over chalk, the impervious clays and over-wet soils, but in the garden most of these conditions can be remedied if trouble is taken. Good loamy soil, burnt earth, mortar rubble, drainage and so forth can be applied to a small area where they are not economic on a large one. Shelter from cold winds is necessary for the choicer types of pear and where walls are planted up the south and south-west walls are usually preferable. One must also remember that pears flower early and since pollination weather may be only a matter of minutes, shelter, by facilitating bee and insect flight, in a cold and windy spring, may easily double the crop.

Type of Tree.

For regular cropping where a number of varieties are

grown the sunny side of a wall, or even a wood fence, are the ideal sites. Branches can be bent down and trained in, thus enforcing moderate growth. Roots are controllable and the necessary check to induce or maintain the fruiting habit is most easily given by root pruning. For several useful varieties the open bush shape (see Plate I), or the pyramid, are quite satisfactory and when worked on the quince stock moderate sized and thrifty specimens will result. Only for the standard tree which is worked on the pear stock, and is usually of a cooking variety, should a large tree be necessary and, since almost all varieties can be grown as a bush or on a wall, the standard is seldom planted in the garden.

Propagation of Pears.

As with apples pears are raised by budding in July–August or by grafting March–April. The only stock of interest to the amateur is the Angers Quince, commercially known as Quince A. There are several varieties of quince hailing from different parts of the Continent, and when one imports stocks it is usual (or perhaps I had better say was usual) to find rogues among them. Of late years the variety Quince C has been used to donate extra fruitfulness or precocity to difficult pears such as Doyenné du Comice, but this stock does not seem to agree with all soils or with all varieties of pear, and stems of trees worked on it are apt to be rough and unsightly. If buying trees on C discard those which have pustuled bark.

Weak Unions.

Many varieties of pear, though they will start off well enough on Quince A, make a weak union which predisposes them to blow away from the rootstocks in windy weather when heavily loaded with fruit. They will also show incompatibility by unequal growth and by the too early colouring of the leaf. To obviate this incompatibility the varieties concerned are what is known as "double-worked," i.e. a variety known to make a sound, strong union with the stock, such as Pitmaston Duchess or Vicar of Winkfield, is first worked on the Quince A stock, and after a season of growth is cut back and the section of stem remaining is worked over to the difficult variety. If, for example, a Quince A stock is budded with Pitmaston Duchess in August 1943, and the resultant shoot from the bud is cut back in April 1945, it can be grafted with a Dr. Jules Guyot pear scion and by the autumn of that same year a maiden Dr. Jules is forthcoming which will not blow off. This weakness hardly affects pears grown against walls but is worth considering when buying trees to plant in the open on a windy site. Nurserymen know, or should know, the varieties which need double-working and must be expected to charge extra for their trouble. Among them are Clapp's Favourite, Jargonelle, Dr. Jules Guyot, Marie Louise, Thompson's and Williams. A friend tells me that incompatible pears become compatible if worked on the Whitethorn stock, but I have no personal experience of this.

Pears worked on pear stock must be allowed plenty of room, and 25 ft. apart for half-standards and 18 ft. for bush trees is none too much. More and more I incline to the opinion that for perfection in all fruits one should allow a distance between each tree, bush or row equivalent to double the expected height. We do not plant on these lines in England, but the Americans do and I fancy their crop per acre with fewer trees is a bigger one than ours.[1] For pyramid or bush trees on Quince A 15 ft. should be the minimum allowed, and 12 ft. may be only entertained where careful and intelligent pruning of branch and roots can be expected.

Since pears spur up well and naturally for fruit-bud they are admirably suited for training as espaliers or cordons both oblique or double-U shape. I have had cordon pears obliquely trained on stone walls in the past 27 ft. long but no more than 5 ft. high, which cropped well and regularly. When planting particular care must be taken to see that the union of stock and scion is well above soil level. If planted too low scion rooting may develop and all dwarfing effect will be lost; indeed the Quince rootstock will dwindle and die, leaving the pear on its own roots which are equivalent in strength to the pear stock.

[1] See note on hand pollination: Chapter XVI, p. 150.

Manuring.

In apples the need for ample potash has been stressed. In pears this is less pronounced but when, after the war, potash is once more available it should not be omitted from the manurial programme. Nitrogen is most needed when trees become over-densely spurred and produce plenty of blossom but little extension growth. Steamed bone flour or raw bone meal are both useful on heavy soils, but where lime is well up can be replaced by superphosphate.

To maintain cropping the following should be adequate: Sulphate of ammonia or nitro chalk $\frac{3}{4}$ oz. per sq. yd., steamed bone or bone meal or superphosphate 2 oz. per sq. yd., sulphate of potash $\frac{1}{2}$ oz. per sq. yd. The first two can be applied in early February and the potash any time in late autumn or early winter.

Regular dressings of compost (for compost making see *Soft Fruit Growing*, Chapter XVIII, a Penguin Special) or farmyard manure can be used in place of artificials. They are best applied as a mulch in spring and turned in during the winter.

Pruning.

Pears will stand a good deal harder cutting than apples, and although certain varieties tend to droop or to carry fruit-bud on the end of lateral and terminal shoots the general tendency under reasonable pruning is to spur up freely with blossom buds. By this I mean that one can more easily train a pear tree into an exact shape than an apple. On the Continent there are many notable examples of fruiting pear trees which have been trained into the shapes of lyres, goblets, cup and saucer, chair and table and so forth. The branches which compose these shapes carry plenty of short fruit spurs, and in due season bear good crops.

To form an oblique cordon, a maiden or one-year-old tree should be planted and for the first three years its extension shoot should be lightly tipped back in winter, removing about a third of its seasonal growth. This tipping will ensure adequate flower-bud and spur development along the stem. After the third year tipping can be omitted. At each winter pruning the cordon should be bent a little lower down by inereasing the slope of the cane to which it is tied.

U cordons and double-U cordons, espaliers and other shapes are formed on the same lines as recommended for apple trees. Bush trees are formed by heading back a maiden tree and allowing three shoots to grow and develop for a year. These are then cut back to two opposed side buds, the branch system is doubled and the following year can be doubled again. As in forming bush apple trees the crowded crotch should be avoided by making sure that the shoot-buds which are produced by the cut-back maiden tree are adequately spaced.

Old trees in the garden which are out of reach of spraying can sometimes be brought back to fruitfulness and freedom from scab by heading them right back and selecting a few of the forest of new growths which will spring out below the point of amputation. Unless, however, these are sprayed with lime-sulphur or bordeaux their very succulence and sappiness predisposes them to severe scab attack.

Summer Pruning.

The pear responds well to summer pruning, and this is really essential to pears grown as trained shapes, cordon, espalier

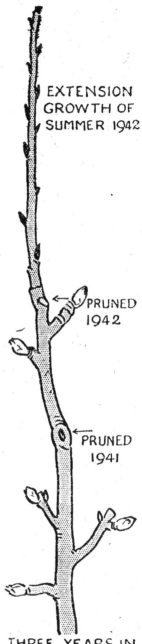

EXTENSION GROWTH OF SUMMER 1942

PRUNED 1942

PRUNED 1941

THREE YEARS IN THE GROWTH OF A PEAR SHOOT
DRAWN FEB. 1943
FIG. 3.

139

and so forth. The simplest method is to wait till the end of July and then cut back all weak side shoots to four leaves and all strong ones to six. Then, in the winter, all these shoots are cut back to two or three buds and the leader shoots reduced by a third. Where natural spur formation is less obvious the short laterals or side shoots can be left unpruned for a year and shortened back to one or two fat blossom buds during the winter.

Bare wood on pear branches is usually due to not tipping the leader shoots hard enough. Excess of spur wood on old trees can with advantage be thinned out in winter pruning, two fat buds on any spur being enough to leave.

Fertilising.

Pears flower earlier than apples owing to the fact that they are of Eastern (probably Syrian) origin. Some varieties are shy croppers by nature, others crop freely and some much too freely. (The variety Fertility is typical of this and has not been recommended, although it is a popular commercial pear, because it combines intense scabbiness with small size and excessive set.) All pears, whether self-fertile or self-sterile, are improved by cross-fertilisation.

It seems curious in view of the fact that the need for cross fertilisation of strawberries was generally recognised by 1830 that the need for this in pears only began to be noticed in 1892, when an American grower observed that better and bigger crops of Williams pears were provided by trees growing near to a few trees of Clapp's Favourite than where Williams were grown by themselves in a block. From this developed the whole theory and practice of inter-pollination. Because of this need you are urged to read, mark, learn and inwardly digest Mr. Crane's tables of suitable varieties to interplant in Chapter XIV.

Thinning.

When a good crop of pears has set and you have satisfied yourself that the larger specimens do not owe their size to the early internal stimulation by pear midge maggots, the crop may be thinned. Do not, however, begin this too soon. Early July is time enough in a normal season.

The size of individual fruits in any variety is determined primarily by the ratio of fine, sound leaves to the number of fruits carried, but each variety has its normal fruit size. Healthy trees can carry big crops of fine fruits because their leaves are able to synthesise a good reserve of elaborated foodstuffs and to lift an adequate supply of water. On a mature tree the number of fruits allowed to a cluster should

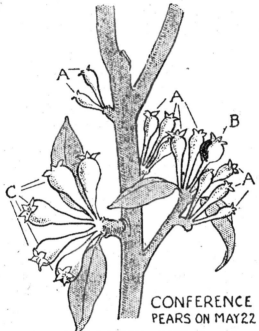

CONFERENCE
PEARS ON MAY 22

PEARS MARKED A ARE INFERTILE AND WILL FALL. B IS ROTTEN AND FULL OF PEAR MIDGE MAGGOTS. PEARS MARKED C ARE FERTILISED AND WILL MATURE.

FIG. 4.

be less in the case of a heavy set than where a vigorous young tree is carrying clusters of fruit on its three-year-old wood and there only. A first crop of Conference, for example, may consist of only half a dozen clusters to a tree, averaging, perhaps, three fruits apiece, and provided growth is good all of them can be allowed to mature. A really heavy set of Conference on a nine-year-old tree may, if unthinned, smash half the branches, especially if cropping has been delayed. The winter's pruning will then include dehorning or severely cutting back the broken limbs to regain rigidity and replace growth. Except, possibly, in the case of such varieties as Marguerite Marillat or Doyenné du Comice there is little advantage in having enormous fruits, and where it is desired to grow these the best place to do so is on wall trees. In such cases a pound weight or one to four fruits, according to size, per square foot of wall should be ample.

Harvesting.

The "mealy" pear is the common lot of the amateur who allows his fruit to ripen on the tree. The highly-coloured pear in the fruiterer's shop, especially when of an early variety, is seldom eatable, early fruit for market sale being usually picked and sent off long before it is coloured or ripe, to avoid this disappointment.

Mealy pears indicate that fruits have been left too long on the tree before being picked. The early and mid-season pears must be picked before the green base colour has warmed to yellow. This means that a variety such as Dr. Jules Guyot, which ripens to a clear lemon, must be picked while quite green. Laxton's Superb pear, Williams Bon Chrétien (plain Williams to most people) and Clapp's Favourite may have actual cheek colour visible on the green (usually brown or brownish red in the case of the first two but definitely red in the last named), but the green base colour must be there with no tint of yellow if they are to travel and mature properly. Picking too early is equally to be avoided, for pears shrivel and again go mealy when immature at picking time.

It is always difficult to know just when to pick pears so that they will ripen to full perfection. In a year such as 1945 the exceptional earliness of Spring and warm weather gave all our fruits an advance which persisted through a cold June and rather wet July so that apples were at least a fortnight earlier than usual, peaches about three weeks ahead of normal, and pears at least as much. In the Thames valley, for example, Laxton's Superb pears were picked on August 21 in 1941, Aug. 11 in 1944 and July 26 in 1945. Because of this variation any date suggestions to follow are useless. One can only judge by the easiness by which the pears will lift off when the fruit is tilted above the horizontal. This means spreading the picking over a week or more. The Americans have a very scientific method of estimating ripeness by testing the degree of hardness; a plunger which records the pressure in pounds needed to force it into the fruit being employed, the pressure figure for each variety being tabulated. The home test is to lift the pear from its vertical angle up to and above the horizontal. Then, if the stalk comes cleanly away from the spur without persuasion or breakage, the fruit is ready. Most earlies should be picked in late July or August, but date of picking will vary with the locality and the season.[1] It is well also to remember that the dates suggested in the list of recommended varieties refer to the southern half of England at around a hundred feet above sea level. Flowering dates and ripening dates are two to three days later for every hundred foot rise, for, though high land escapes the full fluctuation range of temperature, it is definitely lower in general temperature than the low land.

Mid-season varieties, which include such old favourites as Beurré Clairgeau, Beurré Hardy and Beurré Superfin, Conference, Doyenné du Comice, Emile d'Heyst, Louise Bonne, Marguerite Marillat, and Pitmaston Duchess, must be allowed to hang until the fruit, though still green, parts from the spur at a lift to full horizontal, and the crop should be picked over several times and not cleared in one picking since ripening is uneven.

Full colour develops in storage as soon as the green base changes to yellow and brightens the overlaid pink or red. Many varieties have little colour, some are completely russetted, but few remain green when ripe and fit to use. Storage should be dark and cool, a cellar temperature between 40° and 50° F. being ideal. When fruit is brought into a warm living-room it will soon ripen and unless it

[1] Commercial growers picked Conference pears seventeen days ahead of normal in 1943, owing to the earliness of the season.

finishes its ripening in a temperature of 60° F. or so the full flavour and aroma is not forthcoming. Good judges generally agree that to get Comice in perfection one should be prepared to sit up at night. This is, however, an exaggeration and the mid-season to late pears are at their best edible stage over a period of several weeks, so that by bringing in a few at a time to finish off their ripening the season of an individual pear variety can usually be spread over a month or more. Under gas storage it is said to be possible to hold Conference for a period of nine months, but I have never yet eaten a nine-months stored apple or pear with any enjoyment.

Some Useful Varieties.

A glance at Chapter XIV will show that some pears are self-sterile and others self-fertile, but even the self-fertile set more and better fruit if more than one variety is planted so that cross-fertilisation is ensured. If you have room for no more than one pear then Conference should be planted, since it crops heavily alone, and though a proportion of its fruits are apt to come shaped like sausages or bananas for lack of fertile pips they are just as good eating and the variety also lends itself to bottling or cooking. Be sure when peeling or slicing pears for bottling to use a stainless steel knife to avoid discoloration of the fruit.

The Six Best Cooking Pears.

Williams Bon Chrétien (which is the Bartlett pear beloved of American canners), Beurré Clairgeau, Pitmaston Duchess, Vicar of Winkfield, Catillac and Uvedale's St. Germain should suffice.

Twelve Useful Dessert Pears.

To name a dozen pears is easy, but to describe them as the best dozen would be to invite criticism, but few will cavil at a claim for utility. Taken in order of ripening I would suggest Clapp's Favourite, Dr. Jules Guyot, Laxton's Superb, Williams Bon Chrétien, Marguerite Marillat, Beurré Superfin, Beurré Hardy, Conference, Thompson's, Durondeau, Doyenné du Comice, and Winter Nelis. Some few of these are perfect quality pears, others have such attributes as heavy cropping, earliness or lateness.

Pear Varieties Described.
Let us for a moment examine the varieties above, beginning with the dessert.

Clapp's Favourite: Medium to large fruit with smooth skin ripening to pale yellow with bright cherry-coloured stripes and flush. Of very attractive appearance when well-grown. Growth vigorous and upright. Crops regularly and well, but quality is not extra special and the pulp is inclined to grittiness. Will stand lime-sulphur.
Picking time is end of August. Edible soon after.

Dr. Jules Guyot: Grown commercially as supplying a good-sized, attractive dessert pear early in the season. Large when well-grown, ripening to clear pale yellow and very slight flush. Very juicy and has sweetness and a slight flavour. Moderate upright growth. Best double-worked on Quince stock. Will stand lime-sulphur.
Picking time mid to end August. Edible early September.

Laxton's Superb: This medium-sized pear is a cross between Beurré Superfin and Williams and is of excellent quality. Colour very similar to Clapp's Favourite when over-ripe. It will not keep. Upright, moderately vigorous and a regular cropper. Will stand lime-sulphur but is not scabby.
Picking time is end of August. Very edible early September.

Williams Bon Chrétien: Medium size, ripening to yellow with russet and faint red. Extremely sweet, juicy and succulent, with a fine flavour. Growth of moderate strength and able to replace the large annual toll of shoots taken by canker and scab to which it is very addicted. Must be picked green if it is to ripen properly. Will stand lime-sulphur[1] at all stages, and can be grown quite clean of scab.

[1] Although lime-sulphur is recommended for pears in the spraying charts Bordeaux mixture can be used if preferred. Where shoots die off as a result of canker or bacteriosis the Bordeaux is preferable. In seasons of long blossoming, usually cold wet Aprils, one can blow copper-lime dust over the tree with no damage and some fungicidal effect.

Picking time is about end of August. Edible all September, when carefully stored.

Marguerite Marillat: Very large fruit. Pale yellow with bright vermilion flush. Sweet arid very juicy. An upright, rather weak grower on Quince A, and a regular and heavy cropper. Does not suffer from scab unless lime-sulphur spraying is neglected.

Picking season is early September. Good eating mid to end September.

Beurré Superfin: Medium in size, yellow with a patchwork of russet. Very juicy, sweet and free of all grittiness. A first-class pear. Growth is upright and moderate. Should be picked almost before it breaks from the spur and should be eaten just as soon as the stalk end yields to pressure. Will stand lime-sulphur.

Picking time is mid September. Extremely edible through October.

Beurré Hardy: Large to medium. Colour, russet-brown with faint red. Very juicy, flavour good. A strong grower and does well in all shapes. Should be picked before it parts readily from the spur. Will stand lime-sulphur.

Picking time is mid-September. Good eating through October.

Conference: Medium-sized with beautiful tapering shape. When well-grown skin is covered with a clear russet through which show pale green areas becoming solid at the stalk end. A faint pearl on cheek. Rough market samples are merely russet brown and green. Flesh at perfection is pink. Flavour is very good and the pulp is sweet and juicy. A first-class pear, whether for market or the connoiseur. A moderate grower, very free from scab and seldom needing lime-sulphur, with which it is on friendly terms.

Picking time is the last week in September. Excellent eating from early October through November.

Thompson's: Medium to large fruit. Colour pale yellow with some russet. Quality first-class, sweet, juicy, and free of all grittiness. Almost in the Doyenné du Comice class. Tree is a fairly vigorous and upright grower but does not bear with regularity.

PEARS

Picking season is last week in September. Fine eating October and November.

Durondeau: Medium to large. Colour golden yellow with rich brown russet and red beneath. Quality fair, sweet, juicy but not first-class. A good and regular cropper especially on walls. Very much addicted to scab in the open but will stand lime-sulphur. Growth moderate. Picking season is last week of September into October. Fit to eat October and November.

Doyenné du Comice: The pear par excellence. Medium to large. Clear yellow with little russet and some red flush (a bright red cheek when well grown on a wall). Sweet, juicy, melting and altogether delicious. A vigorous grower and not a very regular cropper save on walls. Because of its uncertain cropping should not be largely planted until its performance on the site is known. The best pear variety to plant with Comice to ensure pollination is probably Laxton's Superb. Very liable to scab and will not stand lime-sulphur after blooming. Copper-lime dust can be used as a post-blossom application with no fear of damage. Picking season is first week in October, when a little colour may be present. Superb eating through November.

Winter Nelis: Medium-sized fruit, rather round. Colour greenish yellow and russet. Very delicious, sweet and juicy, with rich flavour. Needs to be worked on vigorous stock, such as pear stock, and is best on a wall. It will ripen slowly and allow a long season of dessert. Will stand lime-sulphur but grown as standard is not usually inclined to scab and should be immune on a wall. Time to pick is early to mid-October. Excellent eating through November, December and well into January.

So much for the dessert varieties, now for the cooking types.

Cooking Pears.

Beurré Clairgeau: This pear is a large, golden brown variety with a reddish flush. It cooks well. A vigorous, upright grower, which crops heavily and regularly. It is grown mainly for market. The tree is rather liable to scab but will stand lime-sulphur.

147

Picking season is at the end of September. In use November and December.

Williams Bon Chrétien: Already described under dessert varieties. The American Bartlett pear, so familiar in cans, is the same variety.

Pitmaston Duchess: Very large, pale yellow with slight russet at the stem end. Fruit can be edible at times and is then sweet, juicy and fair in flavour. It cooks well and is good for bottling. A very strong, vigorous grower making a large standard tree. Liable to scab but will stand lime-sulphur.

Picking time is mid to end of September. Use October and November.

Vicar of Winkfield: Very large, bright green to pale yellow. Cooks well but is not edible as dessert. Makes a good standard and crops regularly. Is very inclined to scab, but will stand lime-sulphur.

Picking time is mid October. Use December and January.

Catillac: Large, almost round and a dull green. Strong grower and a regular cropper. It dates back to the middle of the fifteenth century and has been deservedly popular as a first-rate cooker ever since. Makes a large spreading standard on Pear but can also be grown well on Quince as a bush or pyramid. Will stand lime-sulphur.

Picking time is towards the end of October. Use from February to April.

Uvedale's St. Germain: Enormous fruit, pale yellow and russetted around the eye. Quality is rather poor as the flesh is gritty. Growth very vigorous and fit only for a standard tree. Not recommended save where one is anxious to win a prize for the heaviest pear or to keep them as late as March.

Picking time is October. Use in March-April.

From the details given it will be noted that pears can be eaten as dessert from August till well into January and that cooking varieties can be in use from August until April, a very useful season for so good a fruit. If only dessert pears are grown they are good to cook when picked under-ripe.

PESTS AND DISEASES OF THE PEAR

APPLES and pears share several troubles but one can safely say that in a soil which suits them, and given control of scab, pears are easier to grow than apples. Their unfruitfulness in suburban and other gardens is generally due to their being on the pear stock or to scion rooting, which turns the fruitful dwarf tree into an unduly strong grower. Added to this is the persistent hard pruning, or rather annual beheading to hat pegs, which encourages growth and yet more growth, but practically prohibits fruit-bud production. Insect pests as well as diseases have a great deal to say as to whether or no a fruit crop will be forthcoming even in a year of bounteous blossom. The following are the main pests which attack the pear.

Pear Midge.

You are extremely unlikely to see a pear midge, for it is a very small fly which is about when the first of the pear blossoms are showing white. Her eggs, varying in number from less than a score to as many as thirty, are minute and are laid in the opening buds and flowers, the full count to a single bloom. Having hatched in a few days the little, dirty-white maggots make for the centre of the fruitlet where the embryo pips always seem to exert an attraction. The maggots establish a colony in the centre surrounded with filth and are easily found if you know what to look for. For a time their activity causes a false stimulation to the tissues and the infected fruitlets are outstanding among their fellows in size and apparent promise. When, in early June, fruits show striking variation in size, cut a few open and you will soon know if your pears are suffering from midge. With the fall of the fruitlet in late June to July the maggots leave and enter the soil around the tree, burrowing to a depth of a few inches and later spinning up into cocoons for the winter. Hibernation and soil residence may last one or two years, the main bulk emerging as midges next spring.

Control.

As with all well-entrenched enemies control is not very easy in the egg stage. It can be attacked in the about-to-hatch or just-hatched stage which coincides with full flower development. This stage is at least a week earlier in the flower period of the pear than is the flower stage for the recommended spray for apples against saw-fly, which is at petal fall.

Since the midge maggots, or at least a part of them, are liable to spend two seasons in the soil, hand-picking of the affected fruitlets must be done for two successive years if any abatement is to be expected. This can, of course, only be attempted on cordon, espalier or small bush trees.

An easier method of control is suggested by Dr. Massee of East Malling Research Station, which I found very successful several years ago. This is to keep stirring up the soil around the base of the tree and as far out as beyond the spread of the branches, from the middle of June until the end of July. This stirring up exposes most of the maggots which have gone to ground to bird attack and also discourages them, but to be effective the soil disturbance must be frequent and thorough.

Yet another plan suitable for the garden and relying on exactly opposite procedure is gradually to coat the area where the maggots are likely to be with summer grass mowings from the lawn, repeating the dose until some 3 ins. or 4 ins. depth has been reached. Fermentation rots the grass down to a wet, sodden, impermeable mass through which the emerging fly cannot make her way and she perishes in the attempt.

The latest official method of control is given in the revised Ministry of Agriculture leaflet No. 26, Pear Midge. It is to apply 1 gallon per four square yards of soil of a wash made by adding 1 pint of Tar Oil to 2 gallons of water. This is sprayed or watered on the soil around the tree as the first buds begin to show white very early in April. Trials using D.D.T. in 1945 suggest that this insecticide will soon replace all others, but up to date of revision of this edition details are not forthcoming.

A friend of mine who before World War I grew fruit down at Greenhithe, in Kent, had a large, open space outside his packhouse where several enormous pear trees stood. Every year he lost the crop owing to pear midge, so, being a very wily individual, he pitted his wits against these infernal maggots. His soil was clay and he covered the ground around the pear trees with a thick coating of lime and watered it well. Then he puddled the clay and lime together and let it set. It set so solid that all the pear midge were trapped beneath it. As a result his pear trees set such an enormous crop that the fruit was too small to be saleable. After that having proved his superiority to the insects he bothered no more and let the midges have them.

The Pear Slugworm.

I find many gardeners fail to notice this pest though its damage stares them in the face. When, in late summer, a proportion of your pear leaves show up brown and transparent against the green of undamaged foliage and an inspection shows them to be skeletonised, i.e., the tissue of the leaf eaten out from between the veins, slugworm has been busy. The parent of the slugworm is a saw-fly and once noticed in June when feeding on the leaf as a small, slimy, black object, rather like an immature tadpole, the larva will not easily be overlooked another season.

Control.

This is very simple. As soon as the feeding slugworm is noticed a spray with arsenate of lead at the usual strength of ¼ lb. of dry powder to 25 gallons of water, or even a dust with derris dust, will soon settle it. Occasionally a second brood appears, but this can also be quickly dealt with, though the season may then decide in favour of non-poisonous derris, or D.D.T. dust.

Caterpillars.

Most of the caterpillars affecting apples can also be found on pears from time to time. All are amenable to arsenate of lead in routine sprays as recommended. Occasionally codling moth larvæ will enter pears, and when this does happen it is usually on such a limited scale that the affected fruits can be picked off and destroyed. Many will fall prematurely, and the point of entry is usually through the eye. Sometimes the social pear saw-fly caterpillars will make an appearance. They seem to prefer young trees and the colonies are localised in tents on the same lines as the lackey moth in apples. These can be dragged off with their contents into a bucket with a little paraffin or winter wash in the bottom.

Capsid Bug.

Capsid bugs in variety seem to vary their diet from time to time and the pear is not completely off their menu. If a localised attack does develop and the bitings on the fruit and shoots are identified with an active green bug rather like an aphid, the immediate area can be saturated with a nicotine wash as for apple saw-fly. It is important when attempting to kill capsid to soak the ground after soaking the trees as the little beasts lie doggo till danger is over and then run up the tree again. A D.N.C. petroleum wash in December to February will be worth while if capsid are known to be present.

Birds and Wasps.

Tits will peck holes in pears long before they are ripe and

HOW TO PROTECT FRUITS AGAINST BIRD PECKING

Fig. 5.

bees and ants will do further excavation. This trouble is also common to apples and peaches. One effective way of stopping the damage is to buy small cellophane bags which must be tied tightly at the neck around or just above the base of the stalk. Failing these even newspaper can be tied around fruit and branch. If not tightly tied wasps will still get in. The ripening will continue within the bag. A simpler but much less effective method of prevention is to cut old post cards in half, punch a centre hole and make a cut from the side to the hole with a pair of scissors. The card can then be slid on to the top of the fruit, thus preventing the bird from getting a good stance for its peck. After wet and wind the fruits must be looked over as the cards are apt to soften and blow away.

Fungus Diseases of the Pear.

Pear scab and canker go hand in hand and between them are responsible for more dirty, cracked, useless and prematurely rotten fruit than all the other fungus diseases and pests put together.

Scab on pears is similar to, but not identical with, apple scab. Dr. Wormald, in his excellent book, *Diseases of Fruit and Hops* (Crosby Lockwood & Son, Ltd., London, lists Fertility, Williams, Doyenné du Comice, Beurré Clairgeau, Clapp's Favourite,* Beurré Bosc, Marie Louise* and Beurré d' Amanlis as particularly addicted to scab. (Personally I have not found those marked * very scabby, but once Fertility becomes scion-rooted it is inherently scabby.)

Control.

The life history of scab on pears is so similar to that of apple scab that there is no need to repeat it. It is, of course, a disease of seasonal severity—very much worse in warm, wet weather than in brisk, sunny weather. Sappy growth is always more liable to infection and protective treatment is indicated rather than the attempt to cure an already established attack. The remedies in general use are bordeaux mixture or lime-sulphur before and after blooming at the concentrations advised in the spraying tables. Preventive dusting with copper-lime dust can be used even at mid-bloom and at least one commercial grower of my acquaintance likes to employ this when a wet, cold summer makes for a long period between the white-bud stage and the petal-fall stage. In general bordeaux mixture should not be used later than white-bud stage or damage to fruit by russetting or spotting may result.

Sooty Blotch.

This lowly fungus will also attack pears in a less dense form than apples, but, since the fungus is a product of dank and stagnant conditions, the remedy is to thin out the tree and let in light and air. If bad on otherwise clean fruit the fungus can be removed by a bleach as recommended under sooty blotch in apples. (See Vol. I.)

Canker.

The various apple cankers also affect the pear. Scab infections will attack unripened shoots and over-winter there. The eruption which perforates the bark when the scab spores are taking flight allows entry to the canker spores later. As a result whole branches die back and it is common to see badly attacked trees of Williams carrying a mass of young dead shoots. Very often a single bud here and there becomes infected, dies, and a canker develops around it which ultimately rings the branch, cuts off the sap supply so that the section of the branch above the infection collapses and dies, becoming at once a source of fresh infections.

Control.

The first attempt to control canker must be by the control of scab. Once this is secured the trouble should diminish. Wet soil conditions favour its development and are often responsible for almost uncontrollable attacks. Local canker infections must be cut out or saturated with lime-sulphur solution at about 10 per cent strength to discourage bacterial activity and dead wood must be got rid of. Heavy nitrogenous manuring, or even generous supplies of farmyard manure, should be avoided when canker is present in force.

Brown Rot.

This is a sort of first cousin to canker. The fungus causes whole fruits to rot before they ripen and on the rotten pear circles of dusty, infective pustules will develop. The same fungus is familiar on apples and plums. Fruits which touch an attacked specimen soon rot and whole clusters become involved. Where contact between rotten fruit and young bark on branch or shoot is established infection will soon invade the wood, causing death of the branch above ' the point of infection. Where a rotten fruit falls into the crotch of the tree and stays there the infection may develop in company with canker and a promising young tree may be spoiled, therefore avoid the crowded crotch. (See Vol. I, Chap. VIII, p. 100.)

Control.

While fruit which has dropped on to the ground is less likely to be harmful than fruit which is rotting *in situ* on the tree, the best policy is to remove fruits showing the decay spot before the fungus reaches its fruiting stage (i.e. when the concentric rings of dusty pustules appear). Infected wood and buds killed by the fungus must be cut clean out. Lime-sulphur spraying is to some extent a preventive.

Blossom Wilt.

When the flower trusses suddenly collapse and wither the trouble is usually due to brown rot infection via the flower. Exactly the same type of infection occurs in the case of Morello cherries. There is no remedy for this trouble save the knife and infected shoots must be cut clean away as soon as seen, and burned. Infected wood which is left to over-winter will produce spores which will cause a fresh outbreak next season.

If the above-mentioned diseases and pests are controlled there is usually little else to trouble the grower of pears in the southern half of the country. A warm summer with little rain and plenty of sun is a great asset since it makes for clean well-ripened growth which is resistant to attack.